Everyday
Editing

Inviting Students to Develop
Skill and Craft
in Writer's Workshop

Everyday
Editing

Stenhouse Publishers
Portland, Maine

Jeff Anderson

Stenhouse Publishers
www.stenhouse.com

Library of Congress Cataloging-in-Publication Data
Anderson, Jeff, 1966–
    Everyday editing : inviting students to develop skill and craft in writer's
workshop / Jeff Anderson.
        p. cm.
        Includes bibliographical references.
        ISBN 978-1-57110-709-1 (alk. paper)
        1. English language—Rhetoric—Study and teaching. 2. Editing—
Problems, exercises etc. 3. Report writing—Study and teaching. I. Title.
PE1404.A527 2007
808'.027071—dc22
                                        2007026520

Cover design, interior design, and typesetting by Martha Drury
Art in Figure 9.2 on page 133 by Andrew Schroeder. Used with permission.

Manufactured in the United States of America on acid-free, recycled paper
19 18 17 16 15 14   13 12 11 10 9 8

For all of you who keep me laughing.

Contents

Part I

What Is Everyday Editing?   7

Part II

Acknowledgments

First to my teachers. Thanks to Nancy Roser and Aiden Chambers for continually asking, "What do you notice?" I learned a lot about letting the students engage and lead my classroom with their thinking and questioning. To my seventh-grade English teacher, Ms. Ryan, who taught me that grammar chants can be fun and stored in our brains forever for later use. To Brenda Power, who forever shaped me as a writer; William Varner, whose friendship and banter and intellectual stimulation make life a bit more interesting; and Greg Vessar, whose vigor for teaching and life inspires me. To Nate Butler, whose emails make me LOL; Candace Anderson; Northside ISD and North East ISD; Alana Morris; Leila Christenbury; Dottie Hall; Tracy Winstead; Debbie Grady and the Gates Academy; Janet Angelillo; Harry Noden; and Francis Christensen.

To Gretchen Bernabei, the best writing partner for more than ten years running. I am ready for ten more. Let's do!

Thanks to all my students at Rayburn Middle School. Lola Schaefer, thanks for making my dream to write a children's book a reality, and thank you to all the other authors who give me life and inspire me: Sara Pennypacker, Andrew Clements, and Peter Abrahams.

To the people who support me and nudge me to explore ideas more deeply: the Santa Barbara Writing Project and Sheridan Blau; the Zelda Glazer Institute/Miami-Dade County and Nanette Raska; the North Star Writing Project and Julie Brem and Audrie Wilson; the Harris County Teachers of English and Cindy Benge; University of Houston at Clearlake Writing Project and Charlene Carter; Arcadia Schools; Ilene Anderson; Patti Loper; and Franki Sibberson.

Thanks to the people who believe in my work: Janet Brown at the NCTE consulting network; Phil Fried at Prentice Hall; Lisa Bingen at First Choice; Diane Alsager, Vicki Spandel, Billie Lamkin, Paula Miller, Andrea Dabbs, Eric Tobias, Lisa Rhynes, Rebecca McCarley, Marissa Pena, Melody Collier, Kathy Lyssy, Pedro Chavez, Al and Iris Dodge, Nancy Considine; Joyce and Eddie for pushing me further than I ever thought I could go; and my tireless marketer and Georgia peach, Aimee Buckner.

Thanks to people who make my life fun: Ellen for making sure I take walks; Shelly for reminding me not to worry; and Jayson for the support and laughter.

Why Do My Students Hate Grammar and Editing?

Grammar snobs come in two forms: amateur and pro. Amateur grammar snobs are a lot like amateur gynecologists—they're everywhere, they're all too eager to offer their services, and they're anything but gentle.
　—June Casagrande, *Grammar Snobs Are Great Big Meanies: A Guide to Language for Fun and Spite* (2006)

D o you watch reality shows and correct the participants' grammar, adding the missing *ly*'s to their adverbs?

"My garment fit my model perfect!"

"*LY!*" you yell out at the TV.

Do you silently—or aloud—correct subject-verb agreement? Do you react in glee when you see a sign above a bar door that says ENTERANCE?

Why is it that when you tell most people you're an English teacher, they cover their mouths and continually apologize for "probably saying that wrong"? Do your friends constantly apologize for bad grammar in their emails? Hmm. Go figure.

It's doubt-grammar.

It even plagued TV's Marge Simpson: "In an episode of *The Simpsons*, mother Marge says she wishes she were going to a grammar rodeo. Then she

1

pauses and wonders aloud, 'Or is it, I wish I was going to a grammar rodeo?'" (Casagrande 2006)

Is it subjunctive? Subordinate? What creates all this doubt? It's enough to make a person insubordinate, and more than enough to make kids want to escape editing as much as politicians want us to correct it.

Are students backed into a corner? Are they corrected at every turn, frustrated by their inability to "do it right"? Who wouldn't be turned off to editing? Who *can* catch all of their own errors?

Most adults aren't drawn to things that they don't do well; neither are kids. If you know you have a strong possibility of being corrected, isn't it easier to quit while you're ahead? Do students simplify their writing to avoid making errors, writing only simple sentences?

I recall my French class in college. When I dabbled with more complex constructions or vocabulary, I received many corrections. In fact, the professor took off points for each mistake. If I wrote only simple, banal sentences, I received fewer corrections and higher grades. We don't want to teach kids to cower from complexity, to recoil from risk, to evade experimentation, to pass up play. I don't want to fan the flames of my students' fear that they will never hit the mark for their English teacher.

At the same time, we know editing is testable, even though it may be detestable to our students. But before we decide what we should do to teach editing, we need to ask ourselves an important question: What do standardized tests *really* require? Are we assuming kids will be tested on things they will never be tested on?

We hear the new SAT includes more grammar. Does that mean we teach the parts of speech in the eleventh grade? The seventh grade? Not at all. In fact, editing questions on the SAT, as on most standardized tests, are not based on parts of speech. They don't consist of sentences riddled with errors. They don't include the labeling of grammatical structures.

Standardized tests do ask students to make choices about grammar and editing to make sentences clear and correct. Usually there is only one error to address in each answer choice—there can be only one correct multiple-choice item. Yes, students need the ability to spot errors. Yes, they need to develop the visual acuity and an ear for the flow of language to do so. But how can we do that without making students hate grammar?

And it's not only about what kids are being asked to do on tests. It's also about creating effective writers. *Writing Next* (Graham and Perin 2007), a Carnegie report, summarizes current research on composition instruction. The report specifically addresses the issues of editing and grammar:

> *Grammar instruction in the studies reviewed involved the explicit and systematic teaching of the parts of speech and the structure of sentences. The meta-analysis found an effect for this type of instruction for students across a full range of ability, but surprisingly, this effect was negative. . . . Such findings raise serious questions about some educators' enthusiasm for traditional grammar instruction as a focus of writing instruction for adolescents. (21)*

Writing Next not only tells us what *not* to do, but also advises us what research says does work.

> *A recent study (Fearn and Farnan 2005) found that teaching students to focus on function and practical application of grammar within the context of writing (versus teaching grammar as an independent activity) produced strong and positive effects on students' writing. Overall, the findings on grammar instruction suggest that, although teaching grammar is important, alternative procedures . . . are more effective than traditional approaches for improving the quality of students' writing. (21)*

To keep correctness in its place, some still rely on the pedagogy of the 1800s: Teach editing by correcting and memorizing. The "if-it-worked-for-me" method is often referred to as the traditional approach—a disciplining and training of the mind; teaching correct and socially prestigious forms; memorization and recitation of rules and definitions (Weaver 1996).

Today we associate traditional teaching with sentence diagramming and studying parts of speech. Should we memorize parts of speech? Let's take the word *iron*. Is it a noun or verb? I left the *iron* on yesterday. It's a noun. I *iron* my clothes once a year, whether they need it or not. Now it's a verb. I closed the *iron* gate. Now it's an adjective. This is why many consider the parts of speech "merely notional"(Bryson 1990). This is also why the research tells us to teach function rather than the memorize-and-diagram-and-parse-till-you-drop method.

Tradition.

Whether in the 1800s, 1900s, or the 2000s many think we must focus the bulk of our energy on errors: Look at them, marinate in them, avoid them, fix them, eradicate them. Vicki Spandel (2004) comments on this fervor for faults—this editing-at-all-costs or tough-love mentality: "In their zeal to make everything right, some teachers offer so many corrections and suggestions that all but the most energetic writers feel buried alive." As Dr. Phil would say, "How's that workin' for you?"

What does a traditional approach teach kids about writing? What does a focus on error communicate about the writing process and one's overall success as a writer?

Have you ever gotten back a paper marked up with red-pen marks—or even green-pen marks or another colorful permutation? How did you feel about yourself as a writer? Did you want to write more? Did you immediately, or even later, sit down with a style guide and review your patterns of error and make an action plan on how you'd do better next time? Or did you toss it in the trash or hide it in a folder, since the attempt was obviously a failure? Face it: When students' writing has fallen victim to the red pen, the doubt begins.

The other day my student Ralphie ran up to me in the hallway. "Mr. Anderson, Mr. Anderson, I can't write." Ralphie is a struggling student. I had worked hard to nurture his writing ability, and he was progressing. He had turned an essay in to his developmental reading teacher. She had marked it with more than thirty errors in red, a traditionalist through and through.

"Wait a minute, Ralphie. I know you can write. Let me see it." He handed me the paper. "I like your lead, Ralphie; this is good. You can too write." But Ralphie wasn't having any of it.

"Look!" he said, as if I were dense. "Look at all the marks. I can't write."

"Ralphie, I make errors all the time. That's the writing process. This is a draft."

"No," he interrupted, flipping the paper from front to back, showing me all the marks. "See. I can't write."

Crushing Ralphie's inner writer was not the teacher's intention. That was not the message she intended to send Ralphie. She wanted to make sure he knew what he was doing wrong and that he knew how to fix it. She had good intentions, but she laced them with so many *don'ts*, it turned into a sip of water from a fire hose (Anderson 2005), eviscerating Ralphie's sense of himself as a writer.

She was letting him have it with all the errors, so Ralphie would know all he couldn't do. She envisioned running into Ralphie at the grocery store years from now and him thanking her for being so tough because he learned everything he was supposed to learn. She wasn't doing it to be mean; she felt correction after correction was tough love.

Although it is well intentioned, this practice creates doubt in a writer—as perhaps it did you at some point. Kids develop a fear-driven need to sidestep looking stupid, and often they try to sidestep editing altogether. Kids get the message that, if the teacher's going to edit the paper anyway, why bother doing it yourself? Is that the message we want to send? Are we willing to commit to editing for them for the rest of their lives?

Don't get me wrong. Editing does matter. I don't argue that kids don't need to learn to edit—I just think we can do more than correct sentences to teach editing every day.

What follows is the story I want my writing and editing instruction to tell: students think, write, read, discuss, notice, question, and discover—even during editing instruction. Each lesson in this book is a little chunk of the editing story, a digestible everyday chunk, a part of the editing process that interweaves editing, grammar, and writer's craft, creating both writers and editors.

We actually *teach* students to edit by building concepts through immersion in models, applying the concepts to their own writing while students edit their attempts along the way. We teach editing rather than merely practice it.

But first I want to define what I think editing instruction actually is.

What Is Everyday Editing?

7

What Is
Editing Instruction?

The writer will also discover surprises in the process of editing, and the writer should delight in them.
—Don Murray, *A Writer Teaches Writing* (2003)

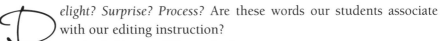elight? Surprise? Process? Are these words our students associate with our editing instruction?

Probably not. Why is that?

We definitely teach students about editing, no matter how we present it in our classrooms. Our attitude, the activities we choose, the way we spend our time—this defines what editing is for our students.

What are we telling them?

Much editing instruction goes something like this. Students attack a sentence on the overhead. Accuracy is not as important as speed. Students know the game. If a teacher puts a sentence on the board, something's wrong with it. It usually has something to do with commas or capitals.

"Delete the comma!"

"Add a comma!"

It doesn't matter that they are guessing. They know they have a fifty-fifty chance of getting the right answer.

Have you ever thought your kids "got it," then wondered the next day why they didn't apply it to their writing? It's a crapshoot—a guessing game. That's not what I want to teach my students. I want to teach them a thoughtful process that may even delight or surprise them.

But how? Should I mark up their papers? If I do, what's that teaching them about editing?

Let's face it: When kids' papers are marked up, they think they can't edit or write. Overwhelmed, students address conventions in a haphazard fashion. Why invest too much? They'll probably get it wrong anyway.

That's not what I want to teach.

Reasoning through decisions about writing and editing takes time: Students need opportunities to test out theories. Correcting doesn't develop— it corrects. And what about the next mistake? How will they know how to fix that? And how will we fix students' attitudes once red-pen thinking takes its toll?

I want students to walk out of my classroom with deep structures and patterns etched in their minds—building pathways, making connections, discovering a way of "thinking" about mechanics' meaning. I want them to celebrate all that what we call editing can do. I want them to celebrate the written word.

We want students to make choices and decisions that create meaning. Not because they're afraid of making an error. Not because of crapshoot-fifty-fifty chances, but because they are thinking. We want them to have ways to reason through what's in front of them, what they see, what it sounds like, looks like, means. A thought process. Yelling random things out at the overhead screen is not thinking.

My Definition of Editing

If we are to believe the posters at the teacher supply store, editing is a phase of the writing process that occurs near the end—after brainstorming or generating ideas, after drafting and revising. Editing, according to these posters, is polishing, cleaning up. We've all seen laminated lists, with their nice, clean boxes waiting to be checked off. The editing items range from checking to make sure your paper has a heading to checking commas (no clarity on why you might need to delete or insert a comma, just a friendly nudge—check commas).

Students need more than a checklist.

Like corrections, checklists don't teach anything beyond what to look out for. When students don't know the patterns, it's just a crapshoot all over again.

Kids aren't professional writers or editors. They haven't yet developed the skills that are listed neatly, all in a row. If only it were that easy. Editing skills need to be taught.

In my classroom, editing is a process. Writing process was founded on the idea that we teach students to do what real writers do. We have to ask: How do real writers edit? Do they have overheads in their offices where they put up transparencies and mark all the mistakes? Lola Schaefer, author of more than two hundred children's books, told me this:

> *I wish I could say that I learned to edit from the many well-executed lessons I received in grammar and high school. But honestly, all of that went in one ear and out the other. I didn't really think about editing and what it meant until I became a writer. Now I'm constantly reading published books with a critical eye, experimenting with punctuation and paragraphing and learning at the knee of an editor. For me, all learning revolves around authentic use.* (personal communication, February 28, 2007)

Another children's book author, April Sayre, said she learned to edit "primarily by wrestling with the process." She edits her writing many times before feeling it is complete. "I have to hear the language in my head and it has to feel right before I can let go of the piece" (personal communication, March 2007). Part of editing is listening to our writing, making it feel right. It takes time. How much class time do our students spend wrestling with the editing process? Is that part of our instruction?

We may not be able to mirror exactly how professional writers edit, but we can discover how they learned to shape their writing, how they learned to craft sentences and meaning.

Many writers say they learned a lot about writing from reading. In the classroom, I experimented to see how I could accelerate students' learning of editing and writer's craft from reading—even with students who are not always natural or voracious readers.

If reading a book or short story teaches professional writers about writing, I wondered if a sentence or two could teach novice writers about craft and mechanics. Could that be editing instruction? I got into a regular habit of spending time reading great sentences and talking about them. And a funny thing happened. The types of sentences we looked at and talked about started affecting their writing. For example, after we looked at a sentence from *Flush* (Hiaasen 2005), the craft and grammar the students focused on in our discussion of the sentence started spilling over into their writing.

The pattern—or process—we discovered looked like this.

I put the sentence up on the board:

The deputy told me to empty my pockets: two quarters, a penny, a stick of bubble gum, and a roll of grip tape for my skateboard.

"What do you notice?" I ask.

"It has a list," Anali offers.

"What's in the list?"

"Stuff in his pocket."

"Like what?"

Students discuss the items in the list. "What does the reader know about the narrator by looking at what's in his or her pocket?" I ask.

"He's probably broke," Diego says, nodding.

"What makes you think that?"

"Well, it says he only has fifty-one cents."

Students talk more about what they know from the sentence without the writer *telling* them. Carl Hiaasen *shows* them with details—a list of details.

"What else do you see?"

"There's that thing with two dots," says Tiffany, squinting.

Pointing to the colon, I ask, "This here? What is that?" We discuss that it's a colon, a sort of drum roll telling us something is coming. In this case, the colon introduces a list.

Later that day, while reading on his own, Jonathan finds a similar sentence. Excited about its similarity to what we discussed, he points to the sentence from *The Higher Power of Lucky* (Patron 2006):

The sun comes out and you look around at all the changes the storm has caused: the outside chairs blown away, the Joshua trees plumped with water, the ground still a little wet.

"Wow, Jonathan! Would you write this on a transparency strip so we can share this tomorrow?" I keep little strips of transparencies in an old tin can, at the ready for my writers.

He returns to his seat, almost gleeful, transparency strip and a Vis-a-Vis pen in hand. Excitement about craft and mechanics is part of successful editing instruction—not dread, not a crapshoot, not red-pen action.

Editing instruction became an editing process. Just as writing process brought joy and clarity to my students' writing, I knew an editing process had begun. All I had to see was all the good writing we shared in literature ripple through their words. When students encountered more and more beautiful text, this joy, this beauty ended up in their writing. And I knew. My students were writing under the influence—of literature, of powerful, effective, beautiful writing. Editing instruction starts with students observing how powerful texts work. What are the writers doing? What can we learn from their effectiveness—and, more often than not, their correctness? This way of editing is inquiry based, open-ended, and bound by meaning:

What do you notice?
What else?
How does it sound when we read it?
What would change if we removed this or that?
Which do you prefer? Why?

These questions put students in the driver's seat. The instruction actually comes from the students. They see what effect the sentence has on them as readers. They see it. They say it. They are the ones commenting on a text's effectiveness, what they notice, not what someone tells them to notice.

Students are not dependent on us for thought. They develop their own thoughts, and we listen and question and shape. Positive words build confidence. That's what I want my children to learn. Confidence. Confidence grounded in knowing.

So if you're still jones-ing for daily transparencies with errors to edit, consider that there may be another way to teach editing: a process that starts with powerful sentences, sentences that teach, sentences that marinate our students in positive models of what writing can be, not what it shouldn't be.

Francine Prose (yes, that's her name) gives this advice about the essentialness of reading "great sentences . . . of great sentence-writers" in her book *Reading Like a Writer* (2006):

One essential and telling difference between learning from a style manual and learning from literature is that any how-to book will, almost by definition, tell you how not to write . . . a pedagogy that involves warnings about what might be broken and directions on how to fix it—as opposed to learning from literature, which teaches by positive model.

The idea is to begin with the end in mind (Covey 2004). Knowing what successful writing looks like (Spandel 2004) helps students produce more effective sentences.

In his book, *Student-Involved Classroom Assessment* (2000), Rich Stiggins talks about how we should put kids in charge of the assessment of their strengths and weaknesses. Students become more independent by doing tasks themselves. If students can see success, they can hit the target.

This is how editing begins in my classroom—with the vision of success and then working backward from there. How do we get to success? How will I welcome students into the world of editing to experiment, play, and learn?

Teaching Editing as a Process of Invitations

An invitation offers something beneficial for consideration. In Purkey and Stanley's National Education Association monograph, *Invitational Teaching, Learning, and Living* (1991), they say, "Learning is most likely to result when students feel confident that they can learn and they look optimistically at their chances for academic success." Can we help students become optimistic about editing? Many students—and teachers—have lost all hope when it comes to editing. Doubt about editing success prevails. Teachers don't think the students are learning and applying what they should, and students think they can't ever do enough.

Messages are sent implicitly and explicitly, from marked-up papers to admonitions: "Did you even read this? Come on, Kelly, how could you spell *when* w-h-e-n-e? How did you get to sixth grade without knowing how to spell *when*?" And sometimes the message is sent to the whole class. "I can't believe the errors I saw in the essays you just turned in. Paragraphs weren't indented and you used apostrophes like you had no idea what they were for. I taught you that. You have no excuse!"

We surrender, throwing our hands in the air.

Students follow suit. When they crumple up their papers or leave them under their desks, they are communicating with us too.

If we nag about everything the kids can't do, students take on an I-can't identity. Would you be encouraged if you were told only what you did wrong? Would you really learn from that or would you shut down? We know that *how* we say things affects kids just as much as *what* we say (Johnston 2004).

When I showed students a powerful sentence, they engaged, became excited, and came alive. When I asked students to imitate sentences, I saw smiles, enthusiasm, and risk-taking. A sentence ended up being a manageable chunk of learning that was easily digested.

I was excited too.

I seized the opportunity to keep the positive momentum going. I began to realize that students needed editing to be shared with an invitational attitude. Could it be that simple? Focus on strengths rather than deficits? I began tinkering with the idea of making editing more invitational, of taking an approach that invites kids in and shows them how the authors did it.

A wonderful thing emerged. We stumbled upon a thinking process that helped students not only change their attitudes about editing, but increase their skills. Together, we learned a thinking process that aided students' decision making. Finally, they edited their own writing because they had the power, not me.

I invite students to notice, to read like writers, to come into the world of editing—a friendly place rather than a punishing place, a creational facility rather than a correctional one. When we develop a place where concepts can be developed and patterns can be learned, kids feel safe, take risks, and feel welcome in every stage of the writing process.

I invite students into editing rather than shutting them out of it. This invitational philosophy undergirds the everyday editing lessons in this book.

2

Why Invite Students
into an Editing Process?

We don't want to confuse mentioning with teaching. Modeling by writing in front of the class, examining writing together, and looking at samples of children's writing is very different from just telling students something and expecting them to go off and do it. Study that is deep and wide accomplishes much more than reminders and nagging ever can.

—Janet Angelillo, *A Fresh Approach to Teaching Punctuation* (2002)

My students helped me discover that teaching editing deeply required a process. In the last chapter, I described the beginning of the process—a powerful sentence. I looked for ways that students could continue to internalize editing concepts and patterns within a process that invited them to ponder, create, read, and notice—that built their confidence and knowing.

After studying brain research and learning theory, I generalized some basic tenets that build effective instruction. This knowledge informed my quest for better editing instruction (Caine et al. 2004; Vygotsky 1986; Piaget and Inhelder 2000; Johnston 2004). Here are four main points that helped me develop my own theories about what editing instruction could be:

- Pay attention to the affective dimension of learning.
- Provide opportunities for social interaction.
- Post, examine, and celebrate powerful models and visuals.
- Focus on patterns that connect rather than rules that correct.

I see these tenets in action in writer's workshop and writing-process instruction. So I began wondering what would happen if this research were applied to the editing part of writing workshop or process instruction. I think the editing step in writing workshop is treated differently to its detriment.

First, I thought about the things kids see around the classroom, such as the posters on the walls and the transparencies projected onto screens.

The editing visuals tend to be corrective rather than exemplary. How could visuals be improved? If we know that kids absorb what they see, why not make it correct or even beautiful? I figured out I could get even more bang for my buck with models of what I wanted the kids to achieve. If I chose well-crafted and correct examples, students absorbed craft and all the things writers edit for.

I thought about how brains search for patterns. At first I wasn't even asking students to imitate the exemplary sentences I posted on the walls or showed on transparencies. When we read, the kids started noticing craft and the mechanics patterns in the texts. When students used these devices and patterns in their own work, they were happy to point it out or beam when someone else did.

This noticing—this effortless, joyful noticing that turned into using and celebrating—led me to the idea to make editing more inviting. I began to put more and more sentences on the board, on charts, and on the overhead, and asking what students noticed, which spilled over into imitation, celebration, combining, revising, and writing. Everything I learned to do instructionally with editing sprang forth from this experience.

Quite simply, the kids showed me what worked.

Together, we noticed how we were surrounded with the ways to make editing work. Every time students or I read a book, we were learning how to edit. We were learning about writing from the masters, using beautiful texts as mentors, zooming in on the parts that made up the whole. It reminded me of some writing advice young-adult novelist Robert Newton Peck (1998) gave on fiction writing. He said that you should write about only what you could see through an empty toilet paper roll. Of course, this helps young writers with focusing, but as Harry Noden shows us all in *Image Grammar* (1999), this zooming in works on sentences too. When we notice what is right and powerful with mentor sentences, we zoom in on a manageable chunk of the writing puzzle, tapping into the flow of syntax and what can be gained from seeing and hearing and thinking about short texts, like mentor sentences.

The children's book *Masterpieces Up Close* (d'Harcourt 2006) takes renowned pieces of art and zooms in on all the little aspects that make up the whole—brushstrokes, detail, and textures. By enlarging and focusing on these aspects of the paintings we see how color, spacing, light, shadow, and texture combine to create the whole piece of art. We toggle between the whole of the painting and back to the small parts that create the beauty, the aesthetic experience.

That's how daily editing instruction could look. We invite students into learning—and it sticks.

Yes, we deal with whole texts—but zooming in on a whole sentence can be very effective. By zooming in, kids can more easily discover the patterns we want them to identify and use: compound and complex sentences, subject-verb agreement, commas, apostrophes, and capitalization. A sentence gives learners a manageable chunk of instruction. Looking at masterpiece sentences "up close" reveals what the little pieces are as well as how we can shape our writing to create the "big picture" of a larger text.

It's far more inviting for students to concentrate on what works in a sentence than to rip one to shreds. After all, writing is an art. Those small details help writing brim with meaning. Looking at sentences *up close* offers students more options for success.

This shift in perspective moves kids' focus from red-pen thinking to *thinking through* editing decisions. When kids see what good writing looks like, they are able to weigh alternatives. For instance, the SAT asks students to choose the best revision of a sentence like the one in Figure 2.1, taken from an online sample.

If we read, analyze, imitate, and edit sentences from literature, then we can tackle questions on standardized tests like this one. The answer is D, but how will students know? How could we teach the concepts a student would need to decide how to solve this question? Editing is a problem-solving process, is it not? But how do we teach these concepts as a meaningful part of the art of sentence making?

What if we look at a sentence like this one from the Newbery Honor book *Rules*? This novel deals with twelve-year-old Christine, who is living with David, her autistic younger brother. She feels she needs to create rules to keep her brother from embarrassing her.

> *Jumping in front of the frozen TV picture, he waves the remote in circles, like it's a magic wand.*
> —Cynthia Lord, *Rules* (2006)

Figure 2.1

> ***Underestimating its value,*** *breakfast is a meal many people skip.*
>
> A. Underestimating its value, breakfast is a meal many people skip.
> B. Breakfast is skipped by many people because of their underestimating its value.
> C. Many people, underestimating the value of the breakfast, and skipping it.
> D. Many people skip breakfast because they underestimate its value.
> E. A meal skipped by many people underestimating its value is breakfast.
>
> A sample item from the SAT asking students to choose the best revision.

"What's jumping in front of the TV?" I ask.

"It's a *who*," Andrew says tentatively.

"Yeah, it's *he*," Jazmin adds.

We discuss how they know and I point out the craft of putting the noun—the *who* or the *what*—near the *-ing* phrase. I move parts of the sentence around so we can discuss the differences and why we make certain choices.

> *Jumping in front of the frozen TV picture, like it's a magic wand, he waves the remote in circles.*

"What changed?" We discuss how now it seems like the TV picture is like a magic wand. Students notice that moving phrases around in a sentence can change or cloud its meaning. We are enforcing the ideas that are tested while learning the craft.

Next, we imitate the sentence and play around with it, moving its phrases and parts to different locations as we did with the sentence from *Rules*. See Figure 2.2 for examples.

Giving attention to effective sentences breaks down editing skills, giving teachers a basic approach that can be used to teach any editing concept or pattern—grammar, usage, mechanics, and craft. The secret is to let students delve into the sentence. The power comes from students telling *you* what they see, exactly what is potent, and answering the question: How did the author do that?

These discussions about writing are social, and provide students an opportunity to test assumptions and apply them. Not only do students want

Figure 2.2

IT'S MOVING DAY:
IS THERE A JANGLER IN YOUR DANGLER?

Hopping in front of the Raspa stand, my brother waves his raspa around, flinging red juice in tiny circles.

Flinging red juice in tiny circles, my brother waves from his raspa, hopping in front of the raspa stand.

Once students have played around with imitating and discussing, the concept and the patterns are forming.

---

to talk, but they will, in fact, often listen more to their peers. By discussing editing in more of a social exchange, kids see they have power, that perhaps it is possible for them to do this writing stuff.

Students cannot edit for items they don't see or hear.

They can't, so they don't. Knowing the underlying patterns is essential for them to see and hear the way language flows and clarifies. Through the language I use in my feedback and instruction, I invite them to believe they can see and hear the patterns.

To accomplish this belief, I start with sentences. Sentences, after all, are chunks of meaning (Anderson 2006). This small chunk of context allows the students *and me* to focus. And if we put a spotlight on such a small chunk of meaning, like a sentence, it should be a well-written one, don't you think? Learners can glean more from well-written sentences, that are correct and effective, than incorrect, crummy sentences. It seems obvious, but then why is correcting sentences as editing instruction so widely used?

Hemingway said, "All we have to do is write one true sentence" (1964). Are the sentences used in your daily practice true? Are they the "truest sentence(s) you know"?

Then comes the next issue: How do we find true sentences? Sentences worthy of such focus? I read attentively, looking for sentences that address patterns or concepts I want my kids to know when they walk away from my classroom. I choose literature that

- connects to students' worlds—their interests, humor, or problems;
- shows a clear pattern that is easy to observe, imitate, or break down;
- models writer's craft and effective writing—powerful verbs, sensory detail, or voice.

To find sentences worthy of zooming in on, simply look at the books you love. They are packed with examples. You don't need certain books; you only need to develop your eye for finding such sentences in any book—or any text, for that matter.

In my search for model sentences, I have almost ruined my reading. I am always thinking, "That's a great compound sentence" or "Kids could easily imitate this sentence."

Instead of reading like a writer, I am reading like a writing teacher.

I do find sentences in any place in any text—but I will let you in on my secret. I dig up most of my mentor sentences in the first few pages of books—sometimes the first line. After all, because authors try so hard to make their beginnings enticing, this is where some of the best writing often is.

Let's take the process of teaching an invitational editing process from start to finish. All the invitations that follow this chapter emerged from the thinking I share with you. Showing students a published or model sentence leads to a discussion of what the writer has done to create his or her sentence, helping students start to develop a writer's eye. The key is to notice the craft of writing at the same time, whether it's sensory details or the use of a comma. How does that word affect your senses? What is that mark doing? How does the meaning or sound of the sentence change if we take that out? My students learn so much from contrasting examples of strong and weak writing. For example, we could look at this sentence from *Made You Look*:

> *His face turned the color of an avocado. He stood motionless, like he was nailed to the floor.*
> —Diane Roberts, *Made You Look* (2004)

After we have talked about the good things the students notice, I say, "What if Diane Roberts had written *He turned green* instead of *His face turned the color of an avocado*"? or "How does the second sentence read differently if I take out the comma?" We read both versions aloud. "Which do you like better? Why?" I am not telling them what they should do; they are identifying and experiencing the difference between stronger and weaker writing. Sometimes we might want to write *He froze*, but sometimes we need the description of the two sentences from *Made You Look*.

Also note that in this exercise I used two sentences. I can break the rules and use more than one sentence, maybe even a paragraph or two. I have to think about what I am teaching and then use the smallest chunk of meaning or context I can find—maybe it's more than a sentence. I just try to keep it as focused as possible. I just couldn't resist these two sentences.

Of course, just *oohing* and *aahing* over good sentences isn't going to make editing happen correctly. It's merely a step in the process, albeit an important one.

Part of the success comes when students try out possible patterns, fiddling with their own sentences and those of others to see what effects they can have on writing. Students crave the power to create different patterns in their writing when they feel safe and their attempts are celebrated. All the while we guide them along, nudging them to try new things.

I needed to see that editing was more than cleaning up copy—though it's that too. It's a process: We see powerful writing, we learn the patterns of craft and grammar, we imitate, combine, uncombine, write, revise, edit. Building concepts—and learning what good writing looks like and sounds like—in the end will make powerful young editors and writers.

Why invite kids into the editing process?

Because editing taught using a more invitational approach deepens students' comprehension of surface features and their significance. And this understanding gives them the power to shape meaning, which is what editing is all about.

The next chapter defines the invitation approach. It is practical, easy to do, and has brought editing and writing success to my classroom.

What Do Editing Invitations Look Like in the Classroom?

Recently she started sneaking grammar (shudder) into the classroom. One day we worked on verb tenses: "I surf the Net, I surfed the Net, I was surfing the Net." Then lively adjectives. . . . She even tried to teach us the difference between active voice—"I snarfed the Oreos"—and passive voice—"The Oreos got snarfed."

Words are hard work. I hope they send Hairwoman to a conference or something. I am ready to help pay for the sub.

—Laurie Halse Anderson, *Speak* (2001)

"What. You'd rather dust than improve your grammar?"

—Rusty's mom in *Swear to Howdy* by Wendelin Van Draanen (2003)

How do we bring grammar into our classroom every day without kids shuddering, like Melinda in the excerpt from *Speak*? How do we weave everyday editing seamlessly into writer's workshop?

Powerful texts serve as the blastoff point for everyday editing. I set the stage and invite kids in to see what sentences can do—to see what they can do. In short, they are invited to think. They are invited to notice. See Figure 3.1 for a few books I've found useful in helping students explore what it means to notice and pay attention to their world.

Figure 3.1

SOME BOOKS WITH CHARACTERS WHO NOTICE

The Other Way to Listen by Byrd Baylor (1997)
Clementine by Sara Pennypacker (2006)
Down the Rabbit Hole by Peter Abrahams (2006)

If I want to teach a concept such as using a comma after an introductory phrase, I display powerful models on the whiteboard, chart paper, or overhead, starting with one and adding others as appropriate with time and student need.

To step inside the decision-making process, students need modeling. As we do in writer's workshop, we model our thinking process aloud. We think and suppose about why the authors made the choices they did, show them how we think it through, providing scaffolds so writers can make their own informed choices.

Inviting Editing and Craft Lessons into Your Classroom

To show how I invite students into everyday editing process, I describe my thinking process in creating each lesson set here. I also share my thoughts and tips for how I envision the process working and my thinking behind the choices I make. Throughout the rest of this chapter, I continue stepping through the process of invitation creation and implementation, interspersing a real example of a lesson set on ways we can punctuate an introductory phrase.

An Annotated Lesson Set: Don't Leave Me Hanging!
Teaching the Use of a Comma After an Introductory Element

This annotated set of editing and craft lessons provides a lens into how invitations for other skills could be added and taught in your classroom. I will describe what I do from creation to invitation followed by lesson pieces and general teaching tips. If you want only the lesson on teaching the use of a comma after an introductory element, simply skip the description.

Once I have decided on a concept for which I'd like to create a series of invitations, I begin paying attention. Much like I ask the students to do in the invitation to notice, I have to start noticing how I see this concept used in real writing. What is it my kids could use the most with this concept or pattern? What would confuse them? How could I break the concept down to its simplest elements? And then I start taking notes, collecting sentences, songs, books, scraps, passages—anything that I can use to immerse my students in writing and in this concept or pattern.

I noticed my students were often creating sentence fragments with introductory phrases—basically using periods rather than commas or nothing at all to separate these phrases from the sentence. I wanted to teach them to set introductory elements off with a comma—a rather useful pattern that students were already using.

While collecting, I found the following sentences. As I read, I marked sentences with a highlighter or a sticky note on the page. If at all possible, I would type them into my computer as soon as possible. I find that I lose many sentences if I do not capture them in some way and corral them together for later use.

You'd think it would be tricky to find sentences that model many different things. It is—but it's not that hard. I scour the first two or three pages or even chapters of books. The benefit is twofold. You will know something about a lot of books, and you will find some great sentences. Additionally, I make sure to write titles, authors, and page numbers—it saves time later. No searching for where the quote came from or who its author is. First, I collect as many sentences as I think have any potential, and later I will decide what to do with them. But I have found that the sentences tell you what they want to teach—and often how I should teach it.

Here are some sentences I came across over a few weeks:

When she took Amy's hand, she was startled by how damp it felt.
 —Scott Smith, *The Ruins* (2006)

When the web is finished, the spider waits for insects to fly into its web.
 —Seymour Simon, *Spiders* (2003)

Before the players begin drills, they must warm up properly.
 —Jeff Savage, *Play-by-Play Football* (2003)

If this were a movie, I'd probably have to kill off my father in the first scene.
 —Paul Acampora, *Defining Dulcie* (2006)

Since I am a picky eater, my mother feeds me peanut butter sandwiches at every meal, including breakfast and midnight snacks.

Before I do anything else, I need to go back over everything that has happened this summer: the Big Mistake, the old man, the book, the lamp, the telescope, and this box, which started it all.
    —Wendy Mass, *Jeremy Fink and the Meaning of Life* (2006)

"If I Had a Million Dollars," a song by the Barenaked Ladies (1992)

I will keep collecting from now until the end of time, but I have enough to get started: a few sentences to notice, imitate, combine, edit, or to spark writing or revision. Sentences need to fill one or all of these possibilities. I always start with the invitation to notice, which doesn't take a lot of preparation. Once you've found a good sentence, slap it up on the overhead and ask kids what they notice. Listen to students' responses and learn. It's an easy initial assessment, and the beauty is that the kids' comments, or lack thereof, cues my next instructional steps.

For example, in the sample lesson interspersed throughout the rest of the chapter, I start with a sentence from *Defining Dulcie*. I chose it because it caught my attention with its bizarreness and its humor, which will get students' attention as well. As I was copying the sentence, I realized it would also be easy to imitate. Already a plan is starting to form—the sentence is leading my lesson.

Invitation to Notice

If this were a movie, I'd probably have to kill off my father in the first scene.
    —Paul Acampora, *Defining Dulcie* (2006)

Once I display the sentence, I ask, "What do you notice?"

Students will have something to say if I can be patient. It's invitational because it's what the students see, not what I tell them to see. Sometimes I am surprised by what they say, and that's okay. It becomes a joy to see what emerges.

"I notice that he uses movie words," Abigail says.

Other kids nod.

"Which words are movie words?"

Figure 3.2

PROBING BEYOND "WHAT DO YOU NOTICE?"

- Craft

  What's working with the text?

  What's effective?

  Where's the good writing? The craft? The effect?

  What else?

- Punctuation

  What's the punctuation doing?

  What effect does the punctuation have on my reading aloud?

  What changes if we remove it? Use something else?

  What's the writer accomplishing with his or her choices?

  What else?

I ask kids "What do you notice?" and "What else?" again and again, listening to their responses, going where they go, making sure we hit on the craft and at least one key point about the patterns in the sentence. We don't have to nor should we cover it all. The invitation to notice is a self-leveling activity in which kids notice what they notice, with slight nudges from time to time.

Students answer: *kill off* (though there is some argument about that), *scene, movie.* "I guess there aren't that many."

"What else do you see?"

"Well, it has one of those . . ." Alex looks around the room for the poster. She's closing in on *apostrophes.* Of course, three students have already said the word, but Alex is going to find it on her own.

"Where's an apostrophe?"

We talk about the sentence, including the comma and how the sentence is not a compound sentence, nor is the comma a serial comma. "Hmm. It is an AAAWWUBBIS."

"What?"

I go on as if I didn't hear the question.

"What's an AAAWWUBBIS?"

"Oh, you know . . . you're not ready yet."

Students are painlessly learning how to analyze text by sharing what they notice about the sentence. Plus I have piqued their interest with a ridiculous mnemonic. I could have told them why the sentence needed a comma, but won't it be better for them to see the pattern develop? When I invite kids to notice, I don't tell them everything they should notice, though I may nudge. Most important, the invitation to notice is about them doing the thinking.

We study models, building our visual and oral stores, noticing what writing is doing. Figure 3.2 offers prompts to help students notice. Taking in, observing, perceiving, becoming aware, detecting, spotting, discerning—this is the beginning of the editing process.

Invitation to Imitate

After I introduce a concept in the invitation to notice, students sometimes need to have a go at imitating the pattern or its effect. They may need to see more examples before they imitate. You can't really do it wrong. We just see what unfolds. We've already collected plenty of sentences; which one do we need to use next? In the case of the *Defining Dulcie* sentence, imitation is the logical next step. To imitate, students look closely at the model, and they in turn clarify their understanding and revise and expand their thinking about the patterns or concepts—editing and craft—as they play with applying what they noticed to their own ideas.

Imitation lets students try on authors' styles and see how they fit within their own developing style. Maybe they will find their own style or combine styles of many authors.

At first kids may not know how to imitate. The more we effectively chunk, model, and unlock sentence patterns with them, the better they will imitate. In addition, we send the message through our actions that editing is about looking inside what writers do, and they feel the success of trying out something small. In so doing, their confidence increases and they are able to do more as time progresses and immediately in the writing they do. See Figure 3.3 for helpful steps for inviting students to imitate.

In this lesson, I see that the sentence was easy for me to imitate, so I quickly share my imitation and map it back to the original. All I have to do is demonstrate how to imitate the pattern and how I can use that pattern to write from my world and experiences. We brainstorm ways we could imitate and change the *if* phrases—we can write a truthful one or make up one.

> *If my dad were a TV star, he'd be Ward Cleaver in* Leave It to Beaver. *He always had to help you see everything about your mistakes. At least that's how it seemed to me.*
> —Mr. A's imitation

Figure 3.3

> ## INVITING STUDENTS TO IMITATE
>
> - Deconstruct the sentence for its prominent features.
> - Show an imitation of your own or a student's and connect back to the prominent features.
> - Show students how to insert their ideas and experiences and still imitate the structure or pattern.
>
> When students are invited to imitate sentences of effective writers, they learn a lot. The time we spend noticing what is strong about the model sentence pays off when kids imitate the punctuation and the writer's craft contained in the sentence.

The best imitation exercises cause more writing. I model this happening and tell kids to go for it when it happens to them. In my class, my students know that if they are deep into what they are writing, they won't get in trouble for continuing to write. I explain to students that getting them writing is the whole point of writing instruction. If they are writing, all is well.

On the board we list all the other *if* possibilities:

If this were a rap song . . .
If my life were a country song . . .
If my life were a video game . . .
If this were a TV show . . .
If this were a comedy . . .
If this were a cop drama . . .
If this were a reality show . . .
If my life were a car . . .
If my life were a movie . . .
If my life were a computer . . .
If my life were a Target store . . .
If this were a basketball game . . .
If this were a football game . . .

After we brainstorm the list, students can play with different sentences in their notebooks, perhaps finding something they want to write about. If they discover they have more to say about one of their invitations, they can; otherwise they are playing with the sentence form. I give about ten minutes, walking around nudging and sharing successes I see.

If kids stop early, I keep trying to send them back to writing. I have to establish at the beginning of the year that we keep writing—no matter what.

I actually have kids ask if they can do more than one imitation—especially if an imitation brims with possibility. I love that. Do they really think I am going to say, "Stop after one, honey. Let's leave some for the other kids to write"? If writing starts to flow, they should learn to go with it—going wherever it takes them.

The next part of the lesson effortlessly flows out of the last. Kids want to share, and sharing is a cause for celebration.

Invitation to Celebrate

Let's face it: The skills that we need to edit effectively are rarely celebrated. More often than not they are approached from a deficit model: What's missing? What's wrong? What needs to be changed? Correction far outweighs celebration. In fact, correction may even stifle, crush, and suffocate celebration.

I like to introduce my students to the idea of celebrating with the picture book *I'm in Charge of Celebrations* by Byrd Baylor (1995). The book teaches us that it is the everyday things that we might forget to celebrate—but that we can celebrate anytime we remember how wonderful everyday things are.

Throughout the writing and editing process, we have to pause and celebrate. This doesn't have to occur at designated times. Celebrating takes place as often as possible—almost all the time. It's that festive attitude I want to cultivate. In an article I wrote for ASCD's *Educational Leadership*, I say, "I'm not saying to go gooey over everything they produce. Be sincere, but also scour, rummage, hunt, and celebrate what is done well—or at least on the path to wellness. These actions will speak loudly: I value what you have to say."

Students share the imitations and stories that came out of them, sparked by a model. It's a time to laugh, to listen, to clap, to praise. Some will keep writing long after you ask them to stop, which is good as well. As students share, I ask them to write their imitations on sentence strips or half sheets of construction paper. Anything. Their creations just have to go up on the walls or in a class notebook. This real audience, this real celebration, gets kids writing and experimenting with editing conventions and it keeps them doing so—in a way that teachers marking up papers all Sunday night never will. Kids will do what we celebrate.

This positive environment will do more to build editing skills than anything else we can do. People like to do things they do well. Think of all the benefits: Kids have their moment in the sun, other students who don't share still benefit from hearing all the effective models, and sharing something so small is nonthreatening and can build trust and community—right away.

Some may keep writing until they feel they have created something they want to share. It's worth the time. Don't leave out the celebration because you have too much to cover. This will make learning stick in a way that coverage of curriculum never will.

"Who has a sentence they'd like to share?"

Sometimes I need to give them as much as eight seconds of wait time, but not today. Hands shoot up.

"If my life were a novella, my sister would be the star. She's always wearing all that makeup and crying all the time," shares Kashmere.

A few kids clap. "Would you read that again, Kashmere?"

After she rereads her sentences, I ask, "What stuck with you in Kashmere's writing?"

This gives kids a chance to treat each other as writers, learning from each other, praising each other. Like all writers, kids need to know what audiences respond to.

Then I ask Kashmere if she'd like to write her sentence on a note card. Of course she does.

The invitation to celebrate isn't about having little plastic champagne cups with sparkling grape juice when we finish a process paper. Yes, celebrating is important, just as it's important for kids to get feedback along the way. It's appropriate, and, I think, essential that we pause and celebrate all the little things. Celebrate often and watch what happens with your young writers. That's right—celebrate what we edit for.

We rode the wave with the *Defining Dulcie* sentence, but it's time to move on. Now I have to think about whether I want to combine sentences next or maybe get the kids writing. Or do my kids need to see more of a variety of sentences to be able to move forward? So, I add a few more sentences to notice, which we may imitate or combine.

At this point I could deluge students with all the ways we can add introductory elements, but I know that I have to start small and add on when kids are ready. Since I started with an *if* sentence, starting with subordinating conjunctions seems the way to go. I have had success in years past intentionally not calling them subordinating conjunctions, by the way. At least at first.

My colleague Cathy Byrd shared with me the AAAWWUBBIS whoop (Anderson 2005). It's said as a word. Yell it in an obnoxious, surprising whoop and you've got it. At the appropriate time, when the students' interest is peaking—which should take a few days—I write the letters on the board, going down the board lengthwise, and then I add the words:

After
Although
As
When
While
Until
Before
Because
If
Since

Sometime later, I will tell the kids that when an AAAWWUBBIS is the first word of a sentence, it causes a comma—AAAWWUBBIS's are regular comma causers. If a sentence starts with an AAAWWUBBIS, you're probably going to need a comma somewhere in the sentence.

Before I do that, I will share some of the sentences I have collected for more invitations to notice—or whatever my kids need or whatever strikes me along the way. It's organic, growing this way and that, a flexible series of invitations. Though I may not use all of the sentences I have collected, I get as many as possible. I can always prune later. Figure 3.4 lists some books about the joys of collecting.

After reading twelve pages, she looked to the end to see how many more pages there were to go: more than two hundred.
—E. L. Konigsburg, *From the Mixed-Up Files of Mrs. Basil E. Frankweiler* (1967)

As the candy cools, the pressurized gas is released and shatters the candy.
—Steve Almond, *Candyfreak* (2005)

As it drew within a few feet of me, it opened its mouth.
—Peter Benchley, *Shark Life* (2007)
(It's fun for the kids to know that Peter Benchley is writing about a shark—and that it's nonfiction.)

As if to welcome them, a half-dozen lights on tall poles flickered to life.
—Lynne Rae Perkins, *Criss Cross* (2005)

Figure 3.4

> ## BOOKS ABOUT COLLECTING
>
> *Donavan's Word Jar* by Monalisa Degross (1994)
> *The Boy Who Loved Words* by Roni Schotter (2006)
> *Max's Words* by Kate Banks (2006)

Although the women's faces are shown from the front, their noses appear in profile to the left. [Describing how Picasso painted people abstractly.]
  —Claire d'Harcourt, *Masterpieces Up Close* (2006)

When you are a kid, you think you are going to remember everything.
  —Esme Raji Codell, *Sing a Song of Tuna Fish* (2006)

When you first gave us this assignment, I thought it was lame.
  —James Howe, *Totally Joe* (2007)

I love the reporter with the totally fake white hair. When something is fake, I want it to look that way.
  —Gail Giles, *Dead Girls Don't Write Letters* (2004)

While I have problems feeling part of my family, I do feel a kinship with our house.
  —Gail Giles, *Dead Girls Don't Write Letters* (2004)

Until the sixteenth century, couples could be married outside a church and without a priest.
  —Claire d'Harcourt, *Masterpieces Up Close* (2006)

Because Ramona wanted to save the best for last, she ate the center of her sandwich—tuna fish—and poked a hole in her orange so she could suck out the juice. Third-graders did not peel their oranges.
  —Beverly Cleary, *Ramona Quimby, Age 8* (1981)

If I stand in a room and no one sees me, it's like I was never there at all.
  —Neal Shusterman, *The Schwa Was Here* (2006)

Since the ink wasn't waterproof, it turned his teeth blue.
—E. L. Konigsburg, *From the Mixed-Up Files of Mrs. Basil E. Frankweiler* (1967)

Since Roy had last seen her, she'd developed deep furrows in her forehead and an angry voice.
—Peter Abrahams, *Nerve Damage: A Novel* (2007)

After I think the kids have been immersed enough in noticing and imitating, I challenge them to try to talk using as many AAAWWUBBIS words to start sentences as possible.

"Since we are trying to learn AAAWWUBBIS sentences (comma!), we are going to try to talk in AAAWWUBBIS sentences," I announce.

"If we keep using the AAAWWUBBIS, *COMMA*, can we leave early?"

"Until I hear everyone trying these out, *COMMA*, I am not going to commit to that," I say. And we go on like this until the end of class.

Remember that the AAAWWWUBBIS has to be the FIRST word of a sentence to cause a comma. As in the sentence *And we go on like this until the end of class*, we don't need a comma when the AAAWWUBBIS comes later in the sentence.

If I can make anything into a mnemonic, I do. Because kids need something to hang on to, they really respond to memory devices like the comma causer, AAAWWUBBIS. Before you stop reading, I will stop using AAAWWUBBIS words to begin my sentences. As you can see, it's quite irritating. Although it's irritating, it does help kids remember. (If that wasn't fun for you, it was for me!)

Invitation to Collect

To clarify an editing concept, kids can delve into texts they're reading to see how authors use the conventions we study.

I may select a text for students to collect from—one I know has an abundance of the particular convention I want to teach. For most editing concepts, I start with a text that is "controlled," meaning I know it has compound sentences or whatever concept I am trying to reinforce. Apostrophes and dialogue are not usually based in author's style; however, sentence construction and patterns can vary greatly from author to author, so I scaffold their collections at first by giving them text where they can find the sentences.

Since authors use various styles, I like knowing we won't encounter countless exceptions when we first try to collect examples for a concept in action. At times, as I do with capitalization collection, I throw caution to the wind and have the students collect in their independent reading. Students can highlight—literally collect—these sentences on an overhead transparency, on strips of paper, or in their writer's notebook. This gives abundant opportunities for reteaching and spiraling in craft and editing concepts, further developing the students' writer's eye.

As I said earlier in the book, not every concept works well as an invitation to collect. Certainly, some thought has to go into this. To begin collecting sentences, I think the kids should have a few weeks of finding what they like. It can be anything. Some will focus on what you have been discussing in class, others won't. We want to cultivate a relishing of language. Starting collections, completely based on students' opinions of what is good, is an excellent way to begin. Plus, as an added benefit, I can use these sentences for later invitations and credit the student who found it. For example, "Anali found this sentence in *Clementine*." Then we notice what the writer is revealing to us about writing.

When inviting to collect, I have to think about how sentences in real books handle concepts. For example, apostrophe hunts go well because every author uses some apostrophes. I have to also think about the point at which I want students to collect during concept building. I may pick a text and copy it, as I do with compound sentences. Or, as in this case, with subordinating conjunctions (AAAWWWUBBIS) beginning sentences, enough writers use them that it's okay to send kids into their personal reading to find a few.

Remember, I only have kids go back and search writing they've already read. I don't want them to stop reading and just hunt for sentences. Students only go back through something they've already read and comprehended. I have done it both ways, and I find this to be the best way. Of course, on the first read some kids will find an exemplary sentence, and I won't stop them, but I just find that they stop reading if they try to do both. That's certainly not what I want.

I begin class by reviewing AAAWWUBBIS. Honoring my seventh-grade English teacher Ms. Ryan, we chant, "*After, although, as, when, while, until, before, because, if, since,*" over and over again. She believed in chants. An AAAWWUBBIS word is a comma causer when it's the first word of the sentence.

I ask kids to return to their reading from the previous day. In our case, it is self-selected reading, but it could be anything that was read recently. They review the text, looking for sentences that start with any of the AAAWWUBBIS words: *After, Although, As, When, While, Until, Before, Because, If, Since.*

When students find a sentence, they write it down in their writer's notebook. After they are collected, we share a few and celebrate the most powerful. Perhaps we write them on the wall to add to our collection of great sentences.

If they don't find any, it's okay. We are just trying to get the concept down. As I walk around the room, I ask some questions to help walk them through a thinking process: Does the sentence start with one of the AAAWWUBBIS words? Is there a comma?

There isn't always a comma after an introductory phrase started with an AAAWWUBBIS, but I wait until a kid asks to fully disclose that. We can discuss the fact that when the introductory information is short and the sentence reads clearly, a writer may or may not use the comma. It's a matter of style and clarity.

At this point, I may continue the collection for a few days, reviewing each day. I put up sentences and ask students what they notice. Now I think they are ready to write.

Invitation to Write

I want to ensure that kids connect the concepts and patterns we study to writing and as another way to express themselves and be understood. Application is where the rubber meets the road. Although invitations to imitate can start the process of attempting, I want to move students back into creating larger texts as soon as possible, zooming in with invitations to notice and zooming back out with invitations to write longer texts (Anderson 2006). I spark a freewrite with literature, challenge students to use a pattern in a draft, ask them to respond to reading, and summarize the day's lesson. Students can apply these concepts in prewriting, drafting, or revision. The students write, but we invite them to try the concept, and we clarify while sharing and conferring.

What I want to stay true to is inviting kids into a conversation about a concept, and giving them opportunities to play around and try the concept. The invitations to write support what I want kids to try or at least give them a context to use for other activities like revision and editing. They also help kids see that this entire editing hubbub is part of writing. Editing: It's not just marking up papers anymore.

For my next AAAWWUBBIS lesson, I want the students to use the AAAWWUBBIS a couple of different ways and explore their usefulness. My colleague Greg Vessar did a variation of one of the lessons from my book

Figure 3.5

WAYS TO INVITE KIDS TO WRITE AND APPLY CONCEPTS

- Imitate a powerful model.
- Try a freewrite.
- Revise a freewrite, adding in the new pattern.
- Respond to or summarize reading.
- Write an exit slip with an example of the targeted concept.

Mechanically Inclined (2005). I used the book *When I Was Little* as the mentor text to kick off an invitation to write, but instead he used the song "If I Had a Million Dollars" by the Barenaked Ladies to get kids writing with subordinate clauses. Music is an effective way to bring kids into writing.

In invitations to write, I look for texts that spark kids' thinking, that connect to them or their world. The text can be essays, excerpts from books, articles, poetry, or even songs.

As I have said, often the invitation to write has elements of the other invitations nudging their way in: an invitation to notice, an invitation to celebrate, and, in this case, an invitation to imitate. Figure 3.5 suggests various ways to invite kids to integrate their new learning into their writing.

When students walk into class, I have the song "If I Had a Million Dollars" playing. A few excited faces enter and a few eyes roll. Before class I did a Google search: "lyrics if I had a million dollars." I got a hit right away. I copied the lyrics and pasted them into a Word document and then altered any grammatical issues I deemed necessary. I paid special attention to the punctuation of the dependent clauses that begin sentences, namely, "If I had a million dollars."

A student passes out the lyrics to "If I Had a Million Dollars."

I stop the music. "Let's just take a minute and listen to this song. You have the lyrics in front of you, so follow along as you listen."

After the song plays, I ask, "What do you notice?"

Students notice some of the details in the song, but Ruben sees those *if* things starting off several sentences.

I ask, "What do you see after those *if* clauses—every time?"

They look back at the lyrics. "Commas."

"Right," I say. "We are going to use this song as a spark." First students brainstorm a list of ten "If I had a million dollars." I show them a few of my own:

If I had a million dollars, I'd buy three new cars.
If I had a million dollars, I'd pay for the first year of college for all my students.

Next, students do their own brainstorming and attempt ten or more. I make sure to tell them to write *If I had a million dollars* COMMA at the beginning of every sentence, and then they tell me what has to follow that comma. Remember, we say "comma" aloud when reading the sentences aloud, but we use the punctuation mark comma when we write.

Students share brainstorming with those at their tables, and then a few share with the whole group. I say things along the way like, "Oh, that reminds me of another idea. I am going to add that to my list before I forget."

After we share and add to our lists, students reread their lists and put a star next to the one or two they have the most to say about, perhaps combining a few that we see a connection among.

Now that students have a topic chosen, they freewrite. But before they write, I challenge them to write their freewrites by starting every sentence with an AAAWWUBBIS word, which means they will probably need a comma. This forces kids to think about the meanings of the subordinating conjunctions and how they connect. Even though I tell kids they don't have to write the AAAWWUBBIS in any special order, several write them in the same sequence in which they appear on the board.

Students share their creations with their groups and then with the class. Some end up like a train wreck, but we're playing, right? Keep it light and marvel at what some of them are able to create in these parameters.

I have found that having kids share with a partner or small group is effective—with the rule that you read your writing instead of merely explaining it. After they have read their writing, others may ask questions or share connections and the writer may talk more about the piece, explaining or elaborating.

Invitation to Combine

This section could just as easily be called "Invitation to Revise." Combining sentences is an effective revision strategy to make writing more concise and connected, and can enhance sentence variety. Many researchers continue to praise sentence combining for helping to develop students' sentence sense. In fact, sentence combining is one of the key recommendations in *Writing Next*

Figure 3.6

GROUP SENTENCE *CRISS CROSS* COMBO

Uncombine the following sentences from *Criss Cross* (Perkins 2005) to make as many sentences as possible:

As if to welcome them, a half-dozen lights on tall poles flickered to life.

Because his burden of garbage was large and precarious, he could not look down at the path and had to go by the feel of dirt under his sneakers.

If Rowanne said something important, something he needed to know, he didn't want to miss it.

Combine the following sentences from *Criss Cross*. Try to use an AAAWWUBBIS word or subordinating conjunction in your combined sentences:

He ate dinner.
Then he headed out to see Phil.
Phil was at his house.

Hector put on his shirt.
Hector slung the guitar over his shoulder.
The guitar belonged to him.
Hector was surprised at how well he had turned out.
Rowanne was surprised at how well he had turned out.

For comparison, the original sentences read:

After he ate dinner, he headed out to Phil's house. When Hector put on his shirt and slung his guitar over his shoulder, he and Rowanne were both surprised at how well he had turned out.

(Graham and Perin 2007). Additionally, my students enjoy it when I uncombine sentences and invite them to combine the ideas and compare their attempts with those of the authors.

When the class was quiet, Gooney Bird began her Monday story.
—Lois Lowry, *Gooney Bird Greene* (2002)

I explain to students that lots of the time we work to combine sentences, but that sometimes we can see combining possibilities more if we work backward. In this invitation to combine, I model uncombining with this Lois Lowry sentence.

Together, the students and I uncombine Lowry's sentence like this:

The class was quiet.
Gooney Bird began her story.
Gooney Bird's story was a Monday story.

Not only are they paying attention to the conventions in Lois Lowry's sentence, but they pay extra attention as they read it again and again—what Gallagher (2004) calls purposeful second draft reading. In addition, they are thinking analytically about meaning. Sentence combining comes with practice, comparing and contrasting other students' combination efforts, and evaluating what makes sense and what's clear.

I give student groups a few sentences to uncombine and few more to combine, challenging them to use an AAAWWUBBIS word in their combination efforts (see Figure 3.6).

Another strategy is to have groups uncombine different sentences and then exchange them with another group to recombine them. Students have fun comparing and contrasting the originals with their recombining. For them it seems more like a game or puzzle than a grammar lesson—nurturing the idea that editing and grammar are ways to play with writing and make sense.

Invitation to Edit

Teachers tell me, "I want my students to look at great sentences, and I want them to edit their writing, but I also need them to get more practice developing a keen eye to find mistakes—in their writing and on tests." I really struggled with meaningful ways to help kids get this practice. I didn't want to use test prep materials. I wanted something authentic, something consistent with all the tenets of effective instruction, but that still gave students an opportunity to meaningfully practice editing, to develop a writer and editor's eye.

As stated earlier, standardized tests usually require students to find an error in a sentence. What's not right? What doesn't work? They don't usually have to identify parts of speech or name grammatical structures. They need to see and hear what is working and not working in writing, whether it's their writing or a test item on a standardized test. How could I stay true to my beliefs and give kids this needed practice? One way I found to do this is an activity called "How'd They Do That?" As with the invitational process, I start with a model mentor text. It may be one we used somewhere in the process. It may be a brand new sentence. The important thing is that the sentences demonstrate writer's craft and the things we edit for. I put a great sentence on the board. We talk about what's good with the sentence. Then I cover the original, correct sentence and reveal another version of it with one thing changed. I mostly change grammar and mechanics, but I also sneak in some craft.

Now we have traveled around all the ways we familiarize ourselves with editing concepts and patterns. Why on earth did I decide to do it in this order? I think it is best summed up by this totally unrelated quote from *The View from Saturday*:

> *How can you know what's missing if you've never met it? You must know of something's existence before you can notice its absence.*
> —E. L. Konigsburg, *The View from Saturday* (1996)

It hit me as the exact way education gets editing instruction wrong. We make it about identifying what's missing or there, and students haven't ever met the concept or become familiar with it. If they don't know of its existence, they can't notice its absence.

I think they have met the AAAWWUBBIS sentence pattern and are ready to edit. Much time has to be spent immersing kids in any concept or pattern before any formal editing takes place. Of course, over time it will naturally flow into instruction, but this invitation to edit does not put so much in front of kids that they may not even know what we're talking about.

I try to move away from the idea of the error hunt to one of looking at how the author created his or her message. How'd he or she do it? How is meaning affected when something changes?

It's a perfect time to mix in other concepts we want to review and touch upon again, but it's all in the context of a well-written sentence. I like to think of editing like a character in *The Astonishing Adventures of Fanboy and Goth Girl* (Lyga 2006)—"It's sort of like dumping the pieces of a puzzle out on the floor, looking at them, and then trying to put it all back together in your head"—making editing something we puzzle over and try to put together, to make sense, to communicate—not avoid error.

> *When the web is finished, the spider waits for insects to fly into its web.*
> —Seymour Simon, *Spiders* (2003)

Figure 3.7

UNCOVERING HOW WRITERS COMMUNICATE WITH READERS

How'd They Do It?

When the web is finished, the spider waits for insects to fly into its web.
—Seymour Simon, *Spiders* (2003)

When the web is finished, the spider waits for insects to fly into it's web.

When the web is finish, the spider waits for insects to fly into its web.

When the web is finished, the spider wait for insects to fly into its web.

When the web is finished the spider waits for insects to fly into its web.

After seeing the correct sentence, students identify what has changed as each sentence is uncovered separately. We are open to changes from sentence to sentence so that the activity continues to be generative.

I hold up the book *Spiders*. "Joshua found this AAAWWUBBIS sentence in the nonfiction book he's reading. I love it when you bring your favorite sentences to me, so that we can use these great sentences that are interesting to look at."

I could insist that all sentences come from fine works of literature. However, I want students to bring in the books they read—they want to read too. I use Newbery books and books I want them to read, but sometimes I need to share what they are bringing to the conversation. It communicates a message about editing and our view of what is important to our students. Maybe there won't be as much to say about these sentences every time, but we are saying a lot by validating their reading and choices.

I take the sentence, type it into a document, then cut and paste it several times. I leave the first sentence alone and then make one change for each following version of the sentence. I may delete or add a comma—anything I want my kids to know (see Figure 3.7).

After this activity I am convinced it's time to move on, but we will keep paying attention to the AAAWWUBBIS pattern. Let the students tell you when it's time to move forward. Teach deeply and kids will know deeply.

$\mathcal{E}$xtending the Invitation

Extending the Invitation lessons are added when the issues come up—exceptions and permutations of patterns and concepts. This is the place for all other things about a concept or ways to stretch and shape it come into play. They may come in before, during, or after the study. When the need arises, it is addressed.

We can point out the AAAWWUBBIS pattern as we come across it. Believe me, kids will point it out for you. When they create AAAWWUBBIS pattern sentences, we celebrate them and post them. Of course, every sentence shouldn't be an AAAWWUBBIS sentence, but they can come in handy when you're connecting two paragraphs. They come in handy when you try to show simultaneous action. And of course, you can do invitations to notice that are what I call combination platters—two or more patterns at once:

> *Before I do anything else, I need to go back over everything that has happened this summer: the Big Mistake, the old man, the book, the lamp, the telescope, and this box, which started it all.*
> —Wendy Mass, *Jeremy Fink and the Meaning of Life* (2006)

> *As he struggles, Max pulls his Swiss Army knife and begins flipping utensils: the fork, the nail clippers, the toothpicks, and . . . a giant Samurai sword.*
> —Gordon Korman, *The Chicken Doesn't Skate* (1998)

AAAWWUBBIS words can start questions as well. These two come from Lily Tomlin:

> *If truth is beauty, why doesn't anybody get their hair done at the library?*
> *If love is the answer, could you rephrase the question?* (2003)

$\mathcal{O}$pen Invitation

Invitations should invite kids into the editing process—that's the point. Anything we can do to communicate encouragement and trust in our students when it comes to editing is on the right track. What we create must do that.

Conversations about what works, conversations about what doesn't work, conversations about what else we could try—all imply to students that they are invited into the editing process.

Since I didn't have room to cram more new stuff into my already crowded language arts and reading block, I wasn't searching for more to do when I created these everyday invitations into editing and writing. I did, however, find ways to combine and refine what I was already doing. I follow some basic patterns teaching editing every day in my classroom. It may not always look like editing, but it is all part of the process of creating editors.

A large portion of everyday editing instruction can take place in the first few minutes of class that, in the past, were reserved for single-sentence corrections on the overhead. Starting every class period with invitations to notice, combine, imitate, or celebrate is an easy way to make sure editing and writing are done every day. I want to communicate with my instruction that editing is shaping and creating writing as much as it is something that refines and polishes it. This brief opener activity that invites students inside writers' heads acts as a meaningful replacement for daily oral language (DOL). I want to step away from all the energy spent on separating editing from the writing process, shoved off at the end of it all or forgotten about altogether.

I want those boundaries muddied so that the rest of the writing and editing lessons I do, besides those start-of-class, blastoff-point invitations, are mixed within mini-lessons, writing, and sharing time in writer's workshop. They aren't merely integrated; editing lessons are the fabric that holds together writing workshop. Editing is not a separate activity, but a part of writing workshop—every day. There is no one time to do any of it. I choose to kick off the class by calling kids' attention to the power of writing, then see where that takes us and connects in writing and reading instruction.

Everyday Editing
Invitations:
10 Lesson Sets

SERIAL COMMA

1

Did You Make the List?
Teaching the
Serial Comma

INTRODUCTION

What you want students to walk away knowing about the serial comma:

- Commas can separate items or actions written in a series.
- Lists consist of three or more items or actions.
- Two items or actions are a pair, not a list, and do not require commas.
- A comma separating the last item in a series may be omitted if *and* or *or* stand in and separate the last item. It's an issue of style.

Misunderstandings you may need to clarify:

- Confusion between lists and pairs
- Assumptions about commas and conjunctions
  —Every sentence that has a comma has a serial comma.
  —Every sentence that has an *and* or *or* has a serial comma.

I connect the serial comma to the power of three. Though lists may have more than three items, most often they consist of, indeed, the magical three.

The three-item pattern feels balanced because we have heard it when we have read aloud our lists for as long as lists have been made. We also heard it in the stories we grew up on: *The Three Little Pigs, Three Blind Mice, Goldilocks and the Three Bears.*

When we look at actions in a series, we have another opportunity to look at agreement, tense, and parallelism.

Say What?

Parallelism is about making things match. If I write a list of actions, each verb should be in the same tense: He *read* a book, *wrote* an essay, and *cleaned* the garage. This polishing point makes a list feel balanced and clear. Working on parallelism can force us to rework our sentences, which is usually a good thing.

INVITATIONS

1.1 *Invitation* to Notice

His room smelled of cooked grease, Lysol, and age.
  —Maya Angelou, *I Know Why the Caged Bird Sings* (1969)

Serial commas are a perfect and useful pattern to kick off a year of writing and learning. Making lists helps students generate ideas. In addition, since I want students to use sensory detail, I hook the concept of the serial comma patterns to those details that make writing zippy. The construction has a purpose. Serial commas help combine sentences and expand ideas by using sensory detail—specific nouns or vivid verbs.

I illuminate Maya Angelou's sentence on the overhead. Pointing to the sentence, I ask students, "What do you notice?"

Destiny says, "It's got commas."

"What are the commas doing?" We read the sentence aloud and discuss the list.

"Sir," Andrew interrupts, "it's got smells."

"It does. Does she say the room smells good or bad?" That brings about an interesting discussion about inferring, showing readers rather than telling. "What if she had just said, 'The rooms smells good' or 'The room smells like stuff'?" While we compare and contrast Angelou's sentences with these other possibilities, students begin to see and name the attributes that make the sentence work. This leads to a discussion about how the list of particular smells lets the reader experience the room. The students discover that lists can be one way to add specifics to our writing.

1.2 *Invitation* to Imitate

Hector's room smelled of gym socks, Hot Cheetos, and lies.
   —Mr. Anderson's writer's notebook

I tell students that this year I will share sentences with them that I like—sentences that work. Sentences we can learn from, and sentences we can imitate. Imitation lets us try on some things powerful writers do that we may never have tried. Here is my imitation of Maya Angelou's sentence: *Hector's room smelled of gym socks, Hot Cheetos, and lies.*

"Let's compare my sentence with Angelou's."

"Well, you both write about smells," Ruben says.

"But you use different stuff," Kayla says.

"Good point," I say. "That's important. I can't use the same things Maya Angelou did. I am imitating—not copying."

"What's the difference, sir?" asks Cerina, squinting her eyes.

"In imitation, I take the pattern of what the writer does, and then I fill in the parts with images from my own mind, my own life." I pick up a marker. "Okay, what's the first thing I did like Angelou?"

"You made it about a room."

I write *Place* on the board (see Figure 1.1). I point to the chunks in both sentences, matching my sentence parts with hers. As we continue our

Figure 1.1

_____ smells of _____ , _____ , and _____ .
(place)   (list of at least three things)

I use this graphic to help students see the underlying pattern we are imitating. I want to show them how we can use a structure to shape our own ideas.

discussion, I keep writing on the board the pattern I imitated and what I filled in. "That's how we imitate."

I sum up our discussion: "I named a place, I used her words *smelled of*, and then I named three things." We may or may not discuss the last item's abstractness. I let kids see what they notice—name brands (proper nouns), lists, things with strong smells, and whatever else they may come up with.

Then I invite kids to try their own imitations, matching structure but adding their own details, which in turn reveal their individual voices. As students write, I play Lynrd Skynyrd's "That Smell" as well as "Senses Working Overtime" by Mandy Moore.

1.3 *Invitation* to Celebrate

I choose to celebrate learning as soon as possible because it is the key to invitational editing: Celebrate what is correct and effective. If my students and I celebrate early and often, positive feelings about editing and views of themselves as writers and editors will blossom. When Andrew smiles and takes pride in his writing, he sees himself as a writer—someone who has the skills to edit.

Students imitate Angelou's sentence and share their imitations aloud with the class. I offer sentence strips to students who share their work. We celebrate, reread, compare, contrast, enjoy, and review craft and grammar.

As students finish their sentence strips, I start taping them all over the walls, on the borders of bulletin boards, on the door, everywhere. I can be choosy later. For now everyone's contributions go on the walls—everyone who wants to have theirs displayed, that is.

More Invitations to Notice and Imitate

Her cleats, shin pads, and sweats were in her backpack, slung over her shoulder and heavy with homework.
  —Peter Abrahams, *Down the Rabbit Hole* (2006)

I walked back to my room wet and dried myself with a pair of jeans. I put on long underwear, pants, a long-sleeved shirt, shoes, and my parka. I stood in front of the heater.
  —Willy Vlautin, *The Motel Life* (2007)

Then I heard a scrape, a thud, and a yelp.
—Byars, Duffy, and Meyers, *The SOS File* (2004)

We had fun with this sentence from *The SOS File* inferring what happened. Of course, we had to read the hilarious short story of a go-kart ride gone wrong before we could go on. After that, we took the idea of listing three sounds for our own sentences, continuing to show rather than tell. The fun comes in trying to make sounds that others will guess. Be prepared, though: Middle schoolers love coming up with sentences that are gross beyond belief. Luke wrote, *I stepped into the yard and heard a wet squish, a strange pop, and a long sucking sound.*

The Old Woman Who Named Things by Cynthia Rylant (2000) also has several sentences that model the serial comma.

1.4 Invitation to Write

The place holds an odor I love. Of wood and stale sweat and chewing gum and more sweat and of the tough rubber skins of all the basketballs ever dribbled here. I breathe deep to take this inside me.
—Tony Johnston, *Any Small Goodness* (2003)

Inviting students to write is where the rubber meets the road. We want to inspire their words to flow. Words can also preserve the things we may forget. We look at Tony Johnston's sentence—how he breathes in his surroundings.

Writers breathe things in and make notes about them. In this way, I target the serial comma pattern and sensory detail. In students' writing, I will ask that everyone try to use at least one serial comma—if not in the draft then in a quick revision after they draft. I don't force them to do anything when drafting, but they can always reenter their writing.

I ask, "What did we learn about writing from Maya Angelou and Tony Johnston?" Kids share things good writers do: Use specific nouns, sensory details, and commas to separate items in a list.

Next, I read a passage from the book *Sing a Song of Tuna Fish: Hard-to-Swallow Stories from the Fifth Grade* (2006) by Esme Raji Codell. "This passage reminds me why we write. Listen for any words or phrases that stick with you."

Let me tell you something.

When you are a kid, you think you are going to remember everything.

You think you are going to remember everyone who sits next to you in class and all the things that crack you up. You think you are going to remember the place where you live and all the things that make your family yours, and not the family down the hall or across the street. You think you are going to remember every punishment and big test and rainy day. You think you will remember how you feel being a kid. You think you will remember so well that you will be the best grown-up who ever lived.

And you might.

Or you might be . . . old enough to get a kind of amnesia. Memories are like days and bones and paper: they can turn to dust, and they change if not preserved.

. . . Who knows? Maybe you can use my stories. Maybe they will help you unpack your own more carefully, just in case the strange and improbable day should arrive that you forget what it was like to be a child.

Though I hope it never does.

—Esme Raji Codell, *Sing a Song of Tuna Fish* (2006)

Codell continues the "Let me tell you something" lead with each chapter. Let me tell you something about my neighborhood or school or mom.

"You get to pick whether your *let me tell you something* is about a person, place, or something of your choosing. The only rule is that you start with the line *Let me tell you something about* _____."

Students write in their notebooks. Afterward we share, celebrating craft and any serial commas and sensory detail that emerge. What we celebrate, we will get more of.

1.5 *Invitation* to Revise

I want my students to get in the healthy habit of reentering their writing. I don't want them only to scratch out writing and never go back to their writing. To start this habit of reentering writing, we have to reread. "As you read your notebook entry, look for places that could use more detail: specific words that stick with the reader, sensory details like smells. Find a place that needs more detail and make a big asterisk right above that." (If kids say, "I don't want to add anything," then just let them know they will do this exercise, but if they don't like the new stuff they come up with, they can choose not to use it—"But I need you to do the exercise. Thank you.")

Students reread their Let-me-tell-you-something freewrite.

After everyone has made an asterisk, kids close their eyes and think about the place or the person they are describing. "Picture the person or place. What do you see?" I pause. "What do you hear? Smell? Taste? Feel?" I pause several seconds between each sense.

Students open their eyes and make a list of at least three things they pictured, smelled, or remembered. If they still haven't found a spot to revise, they make an asterisk over their first sentence. These students can work on leads. Leads are more powerful when they use specific details—lists or not.

We share and celebrate our revisions. Some students don't do stellar jobs. That's not the point. We are helping them see how this comma rule and technique has a life in print that we as writers can use.

1.6 Invitation to Combine

> *I have hair the color of carrots in an apricot glaze, skin fair and clear where it isn't freckled, and eyes like summer storms.*
> —Polly Horvath, *Everything on a Waffle* (2004)

I uncombine the sentence from *Everything on a Waffle*. Then I hand the pieces out to groups and we recombine them:

> *I have hair the color of carrots in an apricot glaze.*
> *My skin is fair and clear where it isn't freckled.*
> *My eyes are like summer storms.*

With sentence combining, I start off simple, knowing we can move into more and more complex constructions as time passes. One of my favorite things about sentence combining is that it is open-ended. The way we combine sentences needs to make sense as well as include the information; however, there is, more often than not, more than one way to do it. And it goes back to one of the most-proven methods of instruction: compare and contrast (Marzano, Pickering, and Pollock 2004). Students compare their creations with others and the original text, evaluating what makes sense as well as where the meaning breaks down.

Since we are working on the serial comma, the three uncombined sentences will easily recombine. We share, compare, and try another sentence.

A single empty chair waited for Rowanne, and a thought whispered from
the back of Hector's mind, but it was drowned out by the sounds of scrap-
ing, shifting chairs.
    —Lynne Rae Perkins, *Criss Cross* (2005)

I show kids Lynne Rae Perkins's sentence and ask them what they notice.
"It doesn't just . . . ," Troy starts. "Never mind."
"What were you going to say? Let's keep figuring this out together," I say.
"Is it still a list?"
"Sort of."
"What do you mean?"
"Well," Troy says, squinting. "It doesn't have three or more things or
smells or whatever."
"Good thinking," I say. "Everyone close your eyes for a second. Let me
reread the sentence and you tell me what you see happening." I reread the
sentence.
"It's these three things that are happening," Daron says.
"So we can have a list of three or more things *or* actions. Let's uncombine
this sentence." The students and I came up with this:

A single empty chair waited for Rowanne.
A thought whispered.
The thought came from the back of Hector's mind.
Hector's thought was drowned out by the sounds of scraping, shifting chairs.

Over the next few days I share more sentences as invitations to notice,
engraining the idea that actions as well as items can appear in a series. I
encourage the kids to collect some sentences and we continue playing with
combining and uncombining sentences.

The sky is clear blue, a light breeze blows from the west, and pale green
water sloshes against the side of the rickety old rowboat that brought us
here.
    —Wendy Mass, *Jeremy Fink and the Meaning of Life* (2006)

Jared Grace took out his red shirt, turned it inside out, and put it on back-
ward. He tried to do the same with his jeans, but that was beyond him.
    —DiTerlizzi and Black, *The Spiderwick Chronicles: Lucinda's Secret* (2003)

I had three places I wanted to visit, six things I wanted to make, and two conversations I wanted to have before dinnertime.
—Katherine Hannigan, *Ida B.* (2006)

1.7 *Invitation* to Edit

I noticed my kids needed some quick editing beyond rereading their larger works of prose. I wanted to train their writer's eyes in quick doses. I experimented with my classes and finally came up with the process described in Figure 1.2.

After printing the transparency with all of the versions of the sentence, I cover all but the first one, the correct version. I ask students what they notice in terms of craft and mechanics. Next, I cover all versions except the one below the first one and ask students what has changed, repeating the covering and asking until the end, when I sum up the learning by showing the correct version again (see Figure 1.3). Students are then invited to reread their writing and notice where they used the same craft.

Figure 1.2

DEVELOPING A WRITER'S EYE WITH *HOW'D THEY DO IT?*

- I show one or more sentences that model craft and the pattern of study, such as serial commas.
- I have the students look at a correct sentence, noticing all it has to offer.
- Then, one by one, I uncover each sentence so that only one sentence at a time is in view.
- I make only one or two changes in each version, training their writer's eyes as their visual memory and acuity are primed.
- Students mentally compare and contrast each version and hypothesize reasons for the choices the writer made in his or her original sentence or sentences.

Figure 1.3

UNCOVERING HOW WRITERS COMMUNICATE
WITH READERS

How'd They Do It?

His room smelled of cooked grease, Lysol, and age.
—Maya Angelou, *I Know Why the Caged Bird Sings* (1969)

His room smelled of cooked grease Lysol, and age.

His room smelled.

His room smelled of cooked grease, lysol, and age.

His room smell of cooked grease, Lysol, and age.

His room smelled off cooked grease, Lysol, and age.

After seeing the correct sentence, students are asked to identify what has
changed as each sentence is uncovered separately.

1.8 *Extending* the Invitation

The gym smells like melting hair spray and aftershave.
—Tony Johnston, *Any Small Goodness* (2003)

We also compare and contrast pairs to clarify the difference. Often students
get the impression that anytime they see an *and* or an *or*, they need a comma.
We look at the Tony Johnston sentence to show that the *and* doesn't cause the
comma or a need for more separation. The *and* serves as the separation in this
pair.

Students revise this Tony Johnston sentence, which describes the school
dance held in the gym, using commas in a series. Of course, they may add or
change detail as long as they rewrite the sentence using a serial comma: *The
gym smells like melting hair spray, sweat, and aftershave.*

While we discuss the choices we made, we again clarify that a list is three
or more things or actions.

I close my fingers around the cool, smooth silver.
　　—Elisa Carbone, *Blood in the River: James Town 1607* (2006)

For clarification on pairs of adjectives, I wait until the issue emerges, and then we deal with it. Two adjectives are sometimes separated by a comma. We also revise the sentence from *Blood in the River* so it reflects a serial comma pattern to highlight the difference: *I close my fingers around the cool, smooth, and valuable silver.*

Sometimes lists are done in different ways: with bullets, outlining, or numbering, like the example from *Becoming Naomi Leon* by Pam Muñoz Ryan (2004):

Chewing on the end of my pencil, I got back to my list, which Gram said was one of the things I did best. I had all kinds of lists in my notebook, the shortest being "Things I am Good At," which consisted of 1) Soap carving, 2) Worrying, and 3) Making lists. There was my "Regular and Everyday Worries" list, which included 1) Gram was going to die because she was old, 2) Owen would never be right, 3) I will forget something if I don't make a list, 4) I will lose my lists, and 5) Abominations. I made lists of splendid words, types of rocks, books I read, and unusual names.

COLONS

2

Here It Comes:
Teaching Colons

INTRODUCTION

What you want students to walk away knowing about colons:

- Colons can introduce lists.
- Colons emphasize to a reader that something important will follow.
- A colon can also introduce a complete sentence.

Misunderstandings you may need to clarify:

- Confusion between colon and semicolon
- Whether or not to capitalize the first word of a complete sentence a colon introduces
- Placing a colon before an incomplete sentence

Say What?

A **semicolon** separates rather than introduces like the colon. The prefix *semi* means "partial," "somewhat," and "half." Semicolons are usually used to separate sentences we want to join without a coordinating conjunction (see "Compound Sentence" lesson). There are occasions when you use a semicolon to separate items in a series. For instance, when items in a list include commas, a semicolon is used to show the separation.

INVITATIONS

2.1 *Invitation* to Notice

The deputy told me to empty my pockets: two quarters, a penny, a stick of bubble gum, and a roll of grip tape for my skateboard.
—Carl Hiaasen, *Flush* (2005)

Colons are not always one of the first things taught, but I think they link ever so well with the list, or serial comma. Colons, in fact, introduce lists. The craft of naming people, places, and things to reveal to readers rather than tell them melds easily with applying the craft of the colon. This unit also acts as a way to review the serial comma.

I put this sentence from *Flush* on the board. "What do you notice about this sentence?" I ask.

"It has a list," Ernesto says.

"It has one of those thingies," offers Ruby. I ask her to come point at the "thingy."

"Yeah, it comes right before the list. Does anyone know what that 'thingy' is?"

After we share our guesses about what the "thingy" is, kids note how naming the items that people or characters carry reveals things about them.

"What do you know about the character?"

I keep the discussion going by continuing to ask, "What else?" until no more answers come.

I sum up our noticings: "Carl Hiaasen didn't tell us the character was a skateboarder or that he didn't have a lot of money. He showed us."

Clarissa adds, "Plus, he gives us clues, like a sheriff telling him to empty his pockets." We get ideas about where the character is and that there must be some sort of conflict.

If a student doesn't relate this passage to the serial comma, I do, comparing and contrasting the two patterns.

Additional Mentor Texts That Reveal Characters or Places Through Lists Following Colons

"Empty your pockets!"

Reluctantly, one by one, Hugo pulled out dozens of objects: screws and nails and bits of metal, gears and crumpled playing cards, tiny pieces of clockworks, cogs, and wheels.

—Brian Selznick, *The Invention of Hugo Cabret* (2007)

But the car is quiet for now, as are the noontime streets: gas stations, boundless concrete, brick buildings with plywood windows.

—Steven D. Levitt and Stephen J. Dubner, *Freakonomics* (2005)

Before I do anything else, I need to go back over everything that has happened this summer: the Big Mistake, the old man, the book, the lamp, the telescope, and this box, which started it all.

—Wendy Mass, *Jeremy Fink and the Meaning of Life* (2006)

I pulled the latch on the mailbox and fanned through the stack of letters: an electricity bill, a New York Times *renewal notice, a bank statement, and a* Bon Appetit *magazine.*

—Tracy Mack, *Drawing Lessons* (2002)

2.2 Invitation to Imitate

The TSA employee emptied my backpack: three books, a journal, and 17 pens.

—Mr. Anderson's writer's notebook

I model how I imitated the sentence from *Flush*. I make sure to match up the chunks of my sentence with Hiaasen's. I write the pattern on the whiteboard:

_____ told me to empty my _____: _____, _____, and _____.

"When I imitate other writers' sentences, trying on their style, I don't use the same content as the writer. I try their structure or the way they put their sentence together." When writers try out other writers' structures, the structure reveals things about the imitator.

To introduce my imitation of Hiaasen's sentence, I explain that I travel a lot. I also have to explain what the TSA (Transportation Security Administration) is and does. Then I ask what the contents of my backpack revealed about me.

Afterward, students brainstorm all the containers that someone could ask them to empty: purse, locker, gym bag, CD case, and pockets. After that, I invite kids to try their own imitations.

2.3 *Invitation* to Celebrate

We take time to celebrate students' creations or what we find in our reading. No matter what stage of the writing process, we pause to celebrate: writing it in a class notebook or binder where we record our successes; recording our imitations on strips of paper or transparencies, sentence strips, or chart paper; or simply reading it aloud.

I also celebrate students who bring me examples of colons found in their reading. In this way, students discover that colons may also introduce a sentence. It's more fun and meaningful when students stumble upon this fact themselves. We celebrate the power to notice and the power to imitate, which cements the use of the colon in our writing and reading.

2.4 *Invitation* to Write

We also enjoyed bragging about which of the penny candies we planned to snap up during our sweet-tooth runs to Suzy's tiendita. Inside the little store, in the presence of the tiny yet intimidating Suzy, we walked around in hushed reverence, debating the intrinsic value of candy cigarettes, wax bottles of sugary "soda water," and pastel necklaces made of sweet-tart gems.

No expert appraiser at Tiffany in New York matched the intense squint of our eyes as we pushed and shoved each other out of the way, gazing hungrily at the tasty jewels encased in round glass jars topped with "fiesta red" lids.

> *Our purchases safely stuffed into little brown paper bags, we explod-*
> *ed onto the dusty callecita of Alice, Texas. With our bare feet, we kicked*
> *up dusty clouds from the road as we walk to our Tia Elia's house, revert-*
> *ing to loud, boisterous "Tejano talk" we seemed to reserve only for mem-*
> *bers of our own family. Oh, the fights over who had made the best pur-*
> *chase. "Mira, mines is more sabroso than yours," a cousin would shout.*
> *Another would counter with, "I'm gonna wear this candy necklace all day*
> *and then eat it after we have Tia Elia's calabaza con pollo. Ay, it looks*
> *like real jewels, right?"*
>
> —Mario Bosquez's *The Chalupa Rules: A Latino Guide to Gringolandia* (2005)

After I have read the passage twice, I ask, "What sticks with you from this passage?" Inevitably, a student repeats the list of candies: "candy cigarettes, wax bottles of sugary 'soda water,' and pastel necklaces made of sweet-tart gems." I remind students that we can introduce lists with colons. We talk about the colon acting like a drumroll, helping writers communicate that something important is coming. I don't discuss that Bosquez didn't use a colon; however, the subject of candy invites the use of a colon to introduce a list.

"When I did my freewrite about candy, I used a colon to introduce a list of candy too." I share my example on the board:

> *I couldn't wait to get my favorite candies at the Sack-n-Pack: fire Jolly*
> *Rancher bars, pixie sticks, and grape Now or Laters.*

> *When it was time to go to the candy store, the hunt for loose change*
> *began: under the couch, between the cushions, beneath Dad's La-Z-Boy*
> *(especially there).*

Students brainstorm more ways to use the colon to introduce a list.

"I was thinking it would be easy to write at least one sentence about candy or a store clerk that uses the colon to introduce a list," I say. "Let's think about Mario Bosquez's excerpt and make a new sentence together."

> *The tiendita was full of valuables: sweet-tart gem necklaces, candy ciga-*
> *rettes, wax bottles of sugary "soda water."*

Students write about a candy, a mean store clerk, relationships with cousins, or anything that connects with them. At this point I don't make them use a colon, but we celebrate students who do.

2.5 *Invitation* to Revise

> *Pop Rocks, for those who have never heard of them, are tiny fruit-flavored candies that come in the shape of finely ground gravel. They're like any other hard candy—a boiled blend of sugar, corn syrup, flavor, and coloring—except for the secret ingredient: carbon dioxide gas compressed at 600 pounds per square inch. As the candy cools, the pressurized gas is released and shatters the candy. But there are still tiny bubbles of pressurized carbon dioxide inside each of the shards.*
>
> *And when the shards melt in someone's mouth, the gas bubbles pop. And I mean pop. Not just some soggy Rice Krispies–type pop, but a sound like fat crackling on a skillet—explosions, actual explosions, which registered seismically in the teeth, particularly if, like me, one decided to chomp down onto the Pop Rocks and not just let them dissolve on the tongue. Not only that, but Pop Rocks tasted good, sweet and fruity, and the different colors (cherry, grape, orange) actually had distinct flavors.*
>
> —Steve Almond, *Candyfreak* (2005)

I read this excerpt to inspire revisions in my students' freewrites. I take time to read the *Candyfreak* excerpt two or three times so that all the powerful language soaks in.

We discuss how the detail lets us reexperience tasting candy. Even if we've never had Pop Rocks, the passage reminds us of how we tasted a candy for the first time or many times. The more specific the detail, the more universal the experience. Students share how we could use the colon pattern to add to our freewrites.

Students reread their freewrites. "Look for places you could use more detail: specific words that will stick with the reader, sensory detail like smells, or naming particular candies," I say. "Find that spot and put a big asterisk right above the spot that needs more detail."

After everyone makes an asterisk, kids close their eyes and think about the place or the person they are describing. "Picture the person or place. What do you see?" I pause. "What do you hear? Smell? Taste? Feel?" I pause between each sense. "Now open your eyes and make a list of at least three things you pictured or smelled or remember now. Go." If they still haven't found a place to add detail, they make the asterisk over their first sentence. Leads tend to be more powerful when they use specific details.

If someone gets stuck, they share their stumbling block with the class. We ask questions and brainstorm solutions, showing students the power of collaboration to solve writing problems. I want my editing and writing instruction to communicate to my students: We are a community of writers who grapple with writing issues together.

2.6 *Invitation* to Edit

How do I send the message that we are studying how writers communicate with their readers and develop kids' visual discrimination abilities—their editor eyes? I came up with an activity called How'd They Do It?

I print a transparency with multiple versions of one sentence (see Figure 2.1). The sentence should be well written and review the concept we are

Figure 2.1

UNCOVERING HOW WRITERS COMMUNICATE WITH READERS

How'd They Do It?

On Saturdays, my cousins and I buy candy from the ice cream truck: sour worms, Jolly Ranchers, and Snickers.
—Mr. Anderson

On Saturdays, my cousins and I buy candy from the ice cream truck: sour worms, Jolly Ranchers, and Snickers.

On Saturdays, my cousins and I buy candy from the ice cream truck.

On Saturdays, me and my cousins buy candy from the ice cream truck: sour worms, Jolly Ranchers, and Snickers.

On Saturdays, my cousins and I buys candy from the ice cream truck: sour worms, Jolly Ranchers, and Snickers.

On Saturdays, my cousins and I buy candy from the ice cream truck—sour worms, jolly ranchers, and Snickers.

After seeing the correct sentence, students identify what has changed as each sentence is uncovered separately. We are open to changes from sentence to sentence so that the activity continues to be generative.

learning, exploring what strategies communicate what to readers. I start the list with one correctly written sentence. Then I cut and paste the sentence below the correct sentence several times, changing one thing each time. I take out craft, punctuation, usage, and grammar. Students describe how the meaning or clarity changes and what we could do to make the meaning clear and effective. I try to change things that I want students to work on. This is one way to sneak in previous concepts or touch on ones that will be covered.

I start by covering up all the sentences except the first, correct version. I ask, "What do you notice?" Next I cover up all versions except the one below the first one, and ask students what has changed. We discuss the change, what effect it has, and how we could make the sentence better—usually returning it to its first version, but not necessarily. I don't want the activity to become pat or too heavily patterned. We should come up with some surprises to see what students' thinking can bring to the sentence.

I repeat the process, covering and uncovering, asking what they notice, the effect of the changes, and what they'd do to improve it. I sum up the learning by showing the correct version again at the end.

Students reread their writing and notice where they used the same craft.

2.7 Extending the Invitation

That semester I was enrolled in seven classes—math, English, shop, history, gym, French, and chicken.
—Gordon Korman, *The Chicken Doesn't Skate* (1998)

Usually a student will find a list in his or her reading that is introduced with a dash. The dash does the same job a colon can do. It says to the reader, "Here comes something!" Comparing the dash to the colon expands students' repertoire. We also talk about a difference between the colon and the dash: You can use a dash almost any way you want. Colons have a lot more rules on how they are used, though. (See 2.8, "Extending the Invitation.") Remind students that we want to use only a dash of dashes. We don't want to overdo anything—do we?

2.8 Extending the Invitation

If students examine colons deeply, they will discover that colons can not only introduce lists, but also introduce complete sentences and quotes. One thing remains the same: The colon acts as fanfare for what follows.

> *Take time for all things: Great haste makes great waste.*
>   —Benjamin Franklin

> *He took his Scout motto seriously: Be prepared.*
>   —Andrew Clements, *A Week in the Woods* (2004)

> *I tried to concentrate on Ms. Meadows's advice: "Just listen to yourself and put it down (on paper)."*
>   —Tracy Mack, *Drawing Lessons* (2002)

> *This was all his life had been since April 29 of last year: a ride to somewhere he didn't want to go.*
>   —Jerry Spinelli, *Eggs* (2007)

The colon may also separate titles and subtitles, as in these four nonfiction books by Jim Murphy:

> *An American Plague: The True and Terrifying Story of the Yellow Fever Epidemic of 1793* (2003b)
> *The Boys' War: Confederate and Union Soldiers Talk About the Civil War* (1990)
> *Blizzard! The Storm That Changed America* (2000)
> *Dugout Wisdom: The Ten Principles of Championship Teams* (2003a)

3

Capitalize on This: Teaching Capitalization

INTRODUCTION

What you want students to walk away knowing about capitalization:

- Proper nouns
  —Specific names of people
  —Specific places such as cities, states, countries, stores, restaurants
  —Brand names
- Proper adjectives
  —Proper nouns used as adjectives
- Titles
  —Books
  —Songs
  —TV shows and movies
  —Poems
- First word of a direct quotation
  —Dialogue
  —Quotes from other works when it's the entire sentence

- Titles used before a person's name
  —Professional titles
  —Government titles
  —Personal titles

Misunderstandings you may need to clarify:

- Confusion about what makes things specific enough for capitalization (wanting to capitalize oak because it's a specific type of tree)
- Students who write in all capital letters (all caps)
- The height ratio between a capital letter and a lowercase letter

Capitalized words denote specificity. Powerful words are specific words creating effective and clear writing. While I teach students to write specifically, I can merge this specificity with capitalization.

Say What?

Titles before names? What do you mean by that? You know *president* becomes *President Martinez* when the title is placed before a name. Combined with a last name like *Jackson*, *doctor* becomes *Dr. Jackson*. However, titles used in a direct address, even when they aren't before a name, are capitalized: *Tell me the truth, Doctor. How long do I have?*

INVITATIONS

3.1 *Invitation* to Notice

Lucky Trimble crouched in a wedge of shade behind the Dumpster. Her ear near a hole in the paint-chipped wall of Hard Pan's Found Object Wind Chime Museum and Visitor Center, she listened as Short Sammy told the story of how he hit rock-bottom. How he quit drinking and found his Higher Power. Short Sammy's story, of all the rock-bottom stories Lucky had heard at twelve-step anonymous meetings—alcoholics, gamblers, smokers, and overeaters—was still her favorite.

> *Sammy told of the day when he had drunk half a gallon of rum lis-*
> *tening to Johnny Cash all morning in his parked '62 Cadillac, then*
> *fallen out of the car when he saw a rattlesnake on the passenger seat bit-*
> *ing his dog, Roy.*
> —Susan Patron, *The Higher Power of Lucky* (2006)

Simply introducing a list of seventeen capitalization rules does nothing to develop my students' power of deduction, nor does it engage them in making sense of what capitalization shows. This activity, based on one found in *Acts of Teaching* (Carroll and Wilson 1993), creates an opportunity to discover the rules within the context of their reading. Since they are engaged in searching, collecting, and collaborating with others to see the patterns, the likelihood that this lesson will stick is great.

Students will see patterns of capitalization within larger texts, categorize the patterns they see, and discover principles of capitalization from the capitalized words in their reading.

First I model the steps of the activity. "We are going to collect some words that begin with capital letters today." I use *The Higher Power of Lucky* passage to model how they will search for capitalized words in their own reading. For the purposes of this activity it is crucial to exclude words that are the first word of a sentence, because any word that is the first word of a sentence is capitalized, which would nullify the patterning and categorizing we want to achieve.

"I notice that the author capitalized *Lucky* and *Trimble*. I exclude the first word of sentences, so I write only *Trimble* on a sticky note with the page number beneath." I keep repeating that we don't use the first word of a sentence so that the message sinks in. Next, I notice aloud that *Dumpster* is capitalized (Dumpster is a trademarked brand name). "Since it is not the first word of a sentence, I write it on another sticky note, including the page number."

Thinking aloud, I encounter *Hard Pan's Found Object Wind Chime Museum and Visitor Center*. "Is this one place?" I ask myself. I read the words again. "It's a museum *and* a visitor center. Since all of these words refer to one place, I will put all the words on one sticky note." I explain that any time words "go together as a unit," I put them all on one sticky note. Then the kids help me finish collecting and recording capitalized words in the passage. Each time we find a word that fits the criteria, we record it separately, unless all the words refer to one thing.

It's also important to note how capitalized, specific nouns add detail to the passage. I contrast a few lines from the passage with the capitalized words deleted, so kids can notice what effect the changes have on the passage. A shift to less specific nouns causes a change in tone and voice.

A girl crouched in a wedge of shade behind the thing. Her ear near a hole in the paint-chipped wall of the place, she listened as a man told the story of how he hit rock-bottom.

I save my sticky notes to continue modeling tomorrow.

3.2   *Invitation* to Collect

Each student needs a novel or nonfiction book at his or her desk. It may be necessary to review capitalization and lowercase letters. A general rule of thumb for students: Capital letters are about twice the height of lowercase letters.

Using novels or any reading materials, students reread several pages they've previously read. As they reread, they collect any words that begin with capital letters—except the first word of sentences. Students write the capitalized words on sticky notes. Each student records five or more capitalized words or groups of words with the page number beneath. Some proper nouns or titles will be more than one word: Rayburn Middle School, *The Real World*, and Dr. Javier Gonzales. Students can write these groups of words on one sticky note. Remind students that if the capital letter starts with a quotation— or dialogue—they may write it down if they put the quotation mark before the word to signal that it is the first word of a direct quotation.

There are only two rules for collecting capitalized words. We exclude any word that is the first word of a sentence. If a word is part of dialogue—we show the quotation marks—or a longer group of words that go together, we record them on one card, as we did with all the words that describe the museum in *The Higher Power of Lucky*. Though this activity will take longer than a few minutes at the beginning of class, it will be far more powerful than a quick look day after day.

While students collect capitalized words and record them on their sticky notes, I walk around clarifying and answering questions. It is amazing how many students need clarification, but don't fret. That's part of concept development. You are helping them clarify for a deeper understanding.

Now I model the next step of the activity, using the words that I had written on sticky notes from *The Higher Power of Lucky*. I place all the sticky notes on the board. "Hmm. I am trying to find ways to group these words. I think there are categories—or words that go together." I move *Trimble* and *Johnny Cash* together. "These are names of people, so those go together. Are there any other words that I could put with these?"

I stand back and put my hand on my chin.

"You could also put Short Sammy with those because that's the name of a person," Marquis offers. I move the sticky note.

"Now, you are going to work with your table groups to combine all your words and find your own categories like we started with my collection."

In small groups, students combine all the sticky notes, placing them faceup on a desk. Students organize words with other like words, discovering categories. I give students new sticky notes to label the categories their group settled on.

Students share their categories, and we record them on the board with a few examples anchoring each pattern. Categories usually include the following:

- names of places, people, cultures
- the pronoun *I*
- titles of books, songs, or any written work (If appropriate, we discuss that in titles we always capitalize the first and last word, but sometimes smaller or less important words are not capitalized if they are not the first or last word of a title. First and last words of titles of written works are always capitalized)
- the first word of a quotation (George Lopez said, "Hey, you have to love capitalization, right?")
- proper adjectives (Chinese food gives me heartburn)
- titles before names (President Lincoln is da bomb)
- initialisms (DVD)

If a category doesn't emerge, I say something like, "Yeah, I was wondering. If I write *Governor Schwarzenegger*, I capitalize *governor*, but if I say *Kanye West wants to be governor*, I don't capitalize *governor*." I lead them to another category: Titles before names are capitalized.

3.3 *Invitation* to Write

When I was nine, my parents borrowed my grandmother's new Ford Mustang because it had air conditioning and because my grandmother insisted, and because there was no way our old Chevy could make the two thousand miles from our house on Mayo Avenue in Houston to Decker, Montana, where my father's old Army buddy owned a sheep ranch. . . . It was the first day after third grade at Pearl Rucker Elementary School,

and I held the bag of peppermints Mrs. Dodge had given me, along with
a note: "Thank you for being my star this year." I didn't like peppermints,
but they were from Mrs. Dodge, and I loved Mrs. Dodge. So my two
younger sisters wouldn't get a single one for the whole drive there and
back. We drew imaginary boundaries on the vinyl seat and dared each
other to cross them.

—Kathi Appelt, *My Father's Summers* (2004)

After I read an excerpt from Appelt's memoir, students share connections
to the reading: trips, riding shotgun, end-of-year happenings, a teacher, parents' friends, or anything they connect with in the reading. "Pay special attention to capital letters as you write," I say.

3.4 *Invitation* to Edit

He was lying in bed, a breeze was blowing through the screened-in porch,
and he was feeling comfortable for the first time in twenty-four hours. It
wasn't so much the heat that bothered him in Manteo, it was the humidi-
ty—sticky, cloying, like swimming through warm chicken broth.

The Greenes had moved to Manteo in November. The weather was
fine throughout winter and spring, but when school let out in June, the
heat wrapped Roanoke Island in the shroud of perpetual humidity. The
only relief came between five and eight o'clock in the morning, when an
Atlantic breeze blew in from the Outer Banks. The best place to catch a
breeze was the screened-in porch overlooking their back yard.

—Roland Smith, *Jack's Run* (2007)

I distribute half-sheets of paper to partners, along with a highlighter. Students
highlight all the words that begin with capital letters and talk about which
pattern they follow, comparing them with the chart of patterns we created in
Invitation 3.3, giving them an opportunity to continue to construct meaning
with exemplary text rather than error-ridden text.

We discuss their findings as a larger group. Then we return to something
we have written previously and highlight all the words we capitalized, as well
as the words we now realize we should have capitalized.

3.5 ℐ𝓃𝓋𝒾𝓉𝒶𝓉𝒾𝓸𝓃 to Edit

The phone rang, but Mack did not get up to answer it.
—Roland Smith, *Jack's Run* (2007)

I print a transparency with multiple versions of the mentor sentence (see Figure 3.1). I start the list with the correctly written sentence. Then I cut and paste the sentence below the correct sentence several times, changing one thing each time. I take out craft, punctuation, usage, and grammar. Students describe how the meaning or clarity changes and what we could do to make the meaning clear and effective. I change things I want students to work on. This way I sneak in previous concepts or touch on ones that will be covered.

I start by covering all the sentences except the first, correct version. I ask, "What do you notice?" Next I cover up all versions except the one below the first one, and ask students what has changed. We discuss the change, what effect it has, and how we could make the sentence better—usually returning

Figure 3.1

UNCOVERING HOW WRITERS COMMUNICATE WITH READERS

How'd They Do It?

The phone rang, but Mack did not get up to answer it.
—Roland Smith, *Jack's Run* (2007)

The phone rang, but Mack don't get up to answer it.

The phone ranged, but Mack did not get up to answer it.

The phone rang, Mack did not get up to answer it.

The phone rang, but mack did not get up to answer it.

The phone rang, for Mack did not get up to answer it.

After seeing the correct sentence, students identify what has changed as each subsequent sentence is uncovered separately. We are open to changes from sentence to sentence so that the activity continues to be generative.

---

it to its first version, but not necessarily. I don't want the activity to become pat or too heavily patterned. We should come up with some surprises to see what students' thinking can bring to the sentence.

I repeat the process, covering and uncovering, asking what they notice, the effect of the changes, and what they'd do to improve each sentence. I sum up the learning by showing the correct version again at the end.

Building on the theory of distance providing clarity ("Put your writing in a drawer for a while"), students reread their previous writing in their portfolios or writer's notebooks. They notice where they used the same craft, as well as shape their text with correct usage.

3.6 *Extending* the Invitation

> *Dad's chain saw cuts a thick branch. It snapped dead at the joint and landed with a thunk at the base of the tree. I was on the back porch steps with Nicky, watching, and trying to draw the tall oak in my sketchbook before it was too late.*
>
> —Tracy Mack, *Drawing Lessons* (2002)

Students often start over-capitalizing after the patterns are discovered. To help with this overcompensation, we discuss that it is just as important to not capitalize words that shouldn't be capitalized. Particular confusions occur over specificity. For example, in the passage from *Drawing Lessons*, students get that *tree* shouldn't be capitalized because it's general; however, they think they should capitalize *oak*. It seems specific to them. Why not *sketchbook*? These conversations can occur over time when discussing writing and reading and in the Invitations to Edit throughout this book.

4

Possession or Contraction—
You Be the Judge:
Teaching Apostrophes

INTRODUCTION

What you want students to walk away knowing about apostrophes:

- Apostrophes show two meanings.
- An *apostrophe s* added to a singular noun shows possession.
- An apostrophe after the *s* in a plural word shows possession.
- Apostrophes also show where letters were removed.
- Words shortened with apostrophes are called contractions.

Misunderstandings you may need to clarify:

- Confusion about any word that ends with an s needing an apostrophe
- Relying on chance rather than meaning with the apostrophe
- Using apostrophes to show pronoun possession

Apostrophes show ownership. They can also show contraction—one or more letters removed can be replaced with an apostrophe. Contractions are considered a more casual style.

Say What?

Through the **years**? There isn't much agreement on whether you use an apostrophe when speaking of years, decades, or centuries. Is it 1800's or 1800s? Both, actually. It depends on the style guide. However, if you are showing possession with a year or century, it always needs the apostrophe: The mullet haircut was 1983's greatest accomplishment.

INVITATIONS

4.1   Invitation to Notice

Harold's eyes were glued to the floor. He couldn't look.
—Dav Pilkey, *Captain Underpants and the Preposterous Plight of the Potty People* (2006)

Apostrophes show who owns what, but they can also indicate some missing letters. This floating comma, as my students often call it, gives writers power to show their readers they know *what* belongs to *whom* and how to shorten a word without an accident.

Setting a context for the sentence, I tell students that Harold is in the principal's office. When I ask what students notice, they point out the strong verb *glued* and address the apostrophes that show both possession and contraction. I want to make sure students hear the key point: Apostrophes show possession or contraction. That's it. If it is showing possession, there must be something for the person or thing to own or possess (an object of possession), and if it is a contraction, letters should be removed or squished out. The apostrophe shows exactly where the deleted letters were.

More Mentors

Over several days, I show students more sentences. Some sentences show how inanimate objects such as the earth can show possession as in *earth's crust*. Kids review many more conventions than the apostrophe when studying mentor texts from professional authors.

Spelda tousled her son's thick black hair.
—Paul Stewart and Chris Riddle, *The Edge Chronicles: Beyond the Deep Woods* (1999)

A great scar in the earth's crust runs for almost 600 miles (960km) along the coast of California. This is the San Andreas Fault, where the Pacific plate slowly grinds along the North American plate.
—Andrew Langley, *Hurricanes, Tsunamis, and Other Natural Disasters* (2006)

Matilda's wonderfully subtle mind was already at work devising yet another suitable punishment for a poisionous parent.
—Roald Dahl, *Matilda* (1998)

Locals say if you go up to "Jacob's Hill," stop on a bridge, put your car in neutral, and turn everything off, your car will roll across the bridge.
—Wesley Treat, Heather Shad, and Rob Riggs, *Weird Texas* (2005)

Alan Ferko's face turned as red as Bo Peep's pigtail ribbons.
—Jerry Spinelli, *Stargirl* (2000)

I begin the discussion of the *it's* versus *its* dilemma and *showing rather than telling* at the same time. To introduce or review these concepts, students compare a scant version of Neal Schusterman's paragraph with the way Schusterman actually wrote. Kids can see that, in the paragraph, *it's* means *it is*.

I don't like her Christmas tree at all.

versus

Don't even get me started about my aunt Rose's Christmas tree. First of all, it's aluminum. Second of all, it's pink. I mean, like the color of Pepto-Bismol, which makes sense, because I get sick to my stomach just looking at it.
—Neal Shusterman, *The Schwa Was Here* (2006)

4.2 Invitation to Collect

I restate what students said about the sentences from *Captain Underpants*, such as the two meanings that apostrophes show. Students search in their reading for a contraction and possessive apostrophe. At first when they search for apostrophes in their reading, I have them record each one on a strip of paper. As they collect, they may ask for clarifications.

"What's *he'd*?" Kashmere blurts out as students are finally quietly looking for apostrophes in their reading.

That's okay. It's a teachable moment. We talk about whether it is ownership or possession, testing each hypothesis, and finally discussing that a contraction can take out more than one letter. It could mean *he had* or *he would*. We reread the sentence, plugging both words in and deciding which makes the most sense, communicating that conventions are about making sense.

If they attempt to use an apostrophe in their writing for the day, students highlight their usage of it in their paper. At the close of class, we celebrate what we've done so far, reading aloud the sentences we found or the ones we've written. The other students listen for the contraction or possessive apostrophe. Can we hear it? We check with the author to see where he or she intended the apostrophe to be. This is the time to clear up misconceptions such as the idea that the apostrophe is caused by *an s at the end of a word*, plural or otherwise.

4.3 *Invitation* to Imitate

Tally's eyes searched desperately for any sign of iron or steel in the cliff.
—Scott Westerfeld, *Uglies* (2005)

When Vanessa shows me this sentence she found with an apostrophe, I think it would be fun to imitate. Plus, it merges into the realm of craft: a character's eyes searching for something. I love that. I start off with my imitation, we break it down part by part, we imitate the chunks, and we change the content as I did in my imitation:

Ellen's eyes darted back and forth as she desperately hoped I'd drop some of my popcorn on the floor.
—Mr. Anderson, writer's notebook

Before you worry too much, Ellen is my dog. And trust me, she's well fed.

Students imitate, we celebrate, and we learn that apostrophes are only one part of the orchestra in fine sentences. Miranda shares her sentence:

Andrew's eyes searched the cafeteria for his girlfriend. Back and forth went his brown eyes. She had disappeared.

Students share and we celebrate.

4.4 Invitation to Edit

It's so dark you can't see your hand in front of your face, let alone the other men around you. You're loaded down with nearly 100 pounds of weapons, food, and equipment.
  —Simone Payment, *Navy Seals: Special Operations for the U.S. Navy (Inside Special Operations)* (2003)

I print a transparency with multiple versions of the mentor sentence (see Figure 4.1). I start the list with the correctly written sentence. Then I cut

Figure 4.1

UNCOVERING HOW WRITERS COMMUNICATE WITH READERS

How'd They Do It?

It's so dark you can't see your hand in front of your face, let alone the other men around you. You're loaded down with nearly 100 pounds of weapons, food, and equipment.
—Simone Payment, *Navy Seals: Special Operations for the U.S. Navy (Inside Special Operations)* (2003)

Its so dark you can't see your hand in front of your face, let alone the other men around you. You're loaded down with nearly 100 pounds of weapons, food, and equipment.

It's dark. You're loaded down with nearly 100 pounds of weapons, food, and equipment.

It's so dark you can't see your hand in front of your face, let alone the other men around you. Your loaded down with nearly 100 pounds of weapons, food, and equipment.

It's so dark you can't see your hand in front of your face, let alone the other men around you. You're loaded down with nearly 100 pounds of weapons food, and equipment.

After seeing the correct sentence, students identify what has changed as each subsequent sentence is uncovered separately. We are open to changes from sentence to sentence so that the activity continues to be generative.

---

and paste the sentence below the correct sentence several times, changing one thing each time. I take out craft, punctuation, usage, and grammar. Students describe how the meaning or clarity changes and what we could do to make the meaning clear and effective. This way I sneak in previous concepts or touch on ones that will be covered.

I start by covering up all the sentences except the first, correct version. I ask, "What do you notice?" Next I cover up all versions except the one below the first one and ask students what has changed. We discuss the change, what effect it has, and how we could make the sentence better—usually returning it to its first version, but not necessarily.

I repeat the process, covering and uncovering, asking what they notice, the effect of the changes, and what they'd do to improve it. I sum up the learning by showing the correct version again at the end.

Building on the theory of distance providing clarity ("Put your writing in a drawer for a while"), students reread their previous writing in their portfolios or writer's notebooks. They notice where they used the same craft, as well as shape their text with correct usage.

4.5 *Invitation* to Write

> *My papa's hair is like a broom, all up in the air. And me, my hair is lazy. It never obeys barrettes or bands. Carlos's hair is thick and straight. He doesn't need to comb it. Nenny's hair is slippery—slides out of your hand. And Kiki, who is youngest, has hair like fur.*
>
> —Sandra Cisneros, *The House on Mango Street* (1991)

"We've been studying the apostrophe, and when I read this story, it made me think about how important apostrophes can be. Sandra Cisneros uses several and she also does a great job with similes. If you don't remember what similes are, see if you do after I read this to you."

I read the chapter "Hairs," from Sandra Cisneros's *House on Mango Street*. After I read the "Hairs" passage twice, I ask, "What sticks with you?"

"Mom's hair smells like bread and the rain falling," Anali says.

"Yeah, I like that too." I reread the sentence. "It has such a wonderful rhythm to it. What else?"

Students share other words and phrases that stuck with them. Sometimes I reread the exact passage from the book. We are celebrating the images that Cisneros created with her words.

Using this passage as a springboard, students write about their families' hair or lack of it. Students write, inadvertently using beautiful similes, such as, "My mom's hair is like a wavy road—black and shining in the hot sun." Who wouldn't celebrate that?

Jonathan rereads his sentence, writing it on a sentence strip, highlighting his use of a simile and an apostrophe. As soon as I ask Jonathan to do this, hands shoot up. Everyone wants to join the fun.

4.6 *Invitation* to Revise

> *Gram had taken to calling me "brown shaggy dog" because of my wild mop and my predisposition to brown-ness (eyes, hair, and skin). I took after the Mexican side of the family, or so I'd been told, and even though Owen was my full-blooded brother, he took after the Oklahoma lot. He did have brown eyes like me, but with fair skin and blond hair in a bowl hair-cut that Gram called a Dutch boy. Due to my coloring, Owen called me the center of a peanut butter sandwich between two pieces of white bread, meaning him and Gram.*
>
> —Pam Muñoz Ryan, *Becoming Naomi Leon* (2006)

Since we've been reading and writing about hair, I bring in another passage from *Becoming Naomi Leon* that describes someone else's hair. After we reread the passage, I ask, "What can we learn from Pam Muñoz Ryan?"

"Her gram or whatever calls her a dog!"

"If my grandma did that, she'd be sorry," Destiny warns.

"Now, now," I say. "But you have a point. What does that reveal about the grandmother, who calls her a shaggy dog?"

"She is not respecting her."

We continue discussing how the author contrasts the family and creates more images of how the whole family fits together and looks together.

Before class, I typed the text from "Hairs." I distribute the text. As students do a quick, silent reread, they highlight any comparison they identify in the text.

Students share their findings with their groups. In this reading, we see how Cisneros uses comparisons or similes to appeal to our senses. "These details add pictures in our heads when we read her writing." We can imitate her style and add details to our writing—comparisons that show rather than tell.

Students reread their "Hair" writing and see if they can add one comparison or highlight any they've already written that are strong. They try to use what they learn from Ryan and Cisneros.

After they reread and highlight their writing, they share some of their successes in groups. Of course, I am at the ready with sentence strips and markers to capture all of the students' good writing for models around the classroom.

4.7 *Invitation* to Collect

Armed with scissors and glue, partners hunt for words that use apostrophes in several magazines and newspapers I have handed out. They find seven. Once they have found them, they create a piece of writing that uses all the apostrophes they have found.

"Plan before you write. How do you think you can use all the words you've found? You are expected to use words from your head too. You will write several words, then plug in one of the words with apostrophes you've cut out." I explain that the goal is for their passages to make sense and for them to use the apostrophes correctly—to show either possession or contraction.

4.8 *Extending* the Invitation

Some stylebooks advise the use of an apostrophe between the decade and the *s* that follows (1700's or 1970's), whereas others advocate against it (1980s or the 1960s). Decide on a style or let both ride. It depends on you, but we have to realize that there are some gray areas when it comes to editing. For example, many years passed before I realized that it was expected to leave just one space after periods. Things change, stylebooks differ, and we have to realize that language is fluid.

5

Is It or Isn't It?
Teaching
Simple Sentences

INTRODUCTION

What you want students to walk away knowing about simple sentences:

- Sentences must have a subject and a verb.
- The sentence questions are the following:
  Who or what did or is something? (subject)
  What did they do? or What are they? (verb)
- Fragments are missing either a subject or a verb.

Misunderstandings you may need to clarify:

- The assumption that a capital letter and a period make a sentence a sentence
- Confusion that an *-ing* verb form doesn't create a sentence: *Students editing* (not a sentence) versus *Students edit* (a sentence)

Simple sentences are the core of it all. They are independent and stand on their own. They are where compound sentences begin and multiply. They are the brick and mortar that hold our writing together. Without them our thoughts would all be fragments. This is a concept that can be taught using the craft of sophisticated word choice and active verbs.

Say What?   **Independent Clauses** have subjects and verbs and stand on their own, making a complete thought. They are everything simple sentences are—synonyms, almost.

INVITATIONS

5.1 *Invitation* to Notice

> *My hair wakes up stupid.*
>   —Tony Johnston, *Any Small Goodness* (2003)

What do we want kids to know in terms of the simple sentence? What will help students survive compound and complex sentences? Students, exposed to a blend of sentences, can discover what makes a sentence a sentence. Then they produce and recognize them with enough proficiency to dabble in compound and complex sentences.

I start with the sentence from *Any Small Goodness*. After we discuss what we notice about it, I ask, "Is this a sentence?"

I get a variety of responses, especially ping-pongy ones ("Yes . . . no . . . I mean, yes"). They watch my face for my response to see which answer is correct. They have no idea. They can speak and write sentences already—much of the time—but can they do so intentionally? Do they know the difference? A sentence may start with a capital letter and end with a period, but it's more than that. It's a fact that on standardized tests, students need to know the difference between a fragment and a sentence. Plus, if they are to write more complex sentence patterns, they need to grasp what really makes a sentence a sentence.

Next, students look at another sentence.

> *My sweat smells like peanut butter.*
>   —Wendy Mass, *Jeremy Fink and the Meaning of Life* (2006)

"What do you notice?"

"Yuck!"

We laugh about Mass's simile—comparing two things we wouldn't usually associate.

I ask, "Is this a sentence?" I model how to think through a sentence. "Who or what smells like peanut butter?" When sentences are broken down like this, students can see that *my sweat* is the subject because that is what smells like peanut butter. "What does the subject—my sweat—do?"

"It smells," they say.

We can either teach *subject and verb* or *subject and predicate*. The point is, we don't get bogged down in labels; we facilitate kids' questioning and thinking about the subject: *Who or what did or is something?* and the verb: *What are they or what did they do?* That's a conceptual level beyond sentences starting with a capital letter and ending with a period. Remember, we can't give students all the exceptions and expect them to develop grammatical concepts. We have to share it in bite-sized chunks, or they simply won't be able to swallow it all.

5.2 Invitation to Edit

> *He paced.*
> *And mosquitoes.*
> *Stacy gasped.*
> *Eric stirred.*
> *And gnats.*
> *Another corpse.*
> *Jeff shrugged.*
> *Amy turned.*
> *To look.*
> *Jeff nodded.*
> *Jeff sighed.*
> —Scott Smith, *The Ruins* (2006)

I make a transparency with published two-word sentences, including a few posers—two words trying to pass themselves off as sentences. I used sentences from a book I was reading at the time, *The Ruins*.

Looking at the transparency, we play a game called *Is It or Isn't It?* In my best game-show-host voice, I say, "It's time to play *Is It or Isn't It?* The game where *you* decide what's a sentence and what's a poser." I explain that those who can explain their answers will compete for the privilege of leaving class one minute early.

"Whoooo can help me review the rules with the contestants?"

Steve's hand shoots up. "It has to answer some questions."

"That's right, Steve." To the class I say, "What are the questions?" I point to the questions that have been posted on the wall for the last few days.

The volunteer explains to the class what the questions are and what the answers show: *Who or what did or is something?* (subject) and *What did they do? or What are they?* (verb).

I read the first sentence, modeling how I reason through it, as this is what the players of the game will do. "*He paced.*" I walk back and forth. "Who or what did or is something? It looks like *he* is the subject. And what did he do?"

The kids blurt, "Paced!"

One by one, volunteers come up and try. If they can identify and explain a poser, they get a bonus point. Remember, we are keeping this light to engage the students and to make grammar less threatening.

5.3 *Invitation* to Collect

Ingrid nodded.
Ingrid awoke.
Ingrid knew.
   —Peter Abrahams, *Down the Rabbit Hole* (2006)

Crawley frowned.
   —Neal Shusterman, *The Schwa Was Here* (2006)

One thing is for sure: Students won't come across a two-word sentence every time they read. So how we collect two-word sentences looks different. Since they are so rare, I start a list on some butcher paper. I invite students to add to the list, if and when they find a two-word sentence. I remind them that the sentence must have a subject and verb to be a sentence.

I also put the two sentence questions on the chart to give the class a place to anchor what a sentence is: *Who or what did or is something?* (subject) and *What did they do? or What are they?* (verb). This shared collection also gives kids another opportunity to test their theories and see how many fragments exist, but we make it clear that this is a way we can identify both. And as a side benefit, they absorb great, active verbs: *shrugs, giggles, grunts*, etc.

Students have to be careful not to identify dialogue tags as sentences; the dialogue tags are only part of the sentences with dialogue.

5.4 *Invitation* to Notice

I read aloud the picture book *An Island Grows*, by Lola M. Schaefer (2006). After I finish reading, I ask, "What do you notice?"

Of course, they notice the rhymes (rhyming couplets), and that the text explains how an island grows, from volcano to the vegetation to the arrival of inhabitants. Before the lesson, I typed the text of the picture book and made copies. I hand out the copies.

"The sentences are short," Lauren observes.

"They sure are—poetic, in fact. How did you know they were sentences?" Students give several of the sentences the sentence test. Then partners highlight all the verbs, closing the discussion by talking about how the verbs are powerful and lively. In two words, the sentences say a lot. We talk about the craft of well-chosen words and how we can think about the words we use, especially specific nouns and lively verbs.

5.5 *Invitation* to Imitate

Stone breaks.
Water quakes.
Magma glows.
Volcano blows.
　　—Lola M. Schaefer, *An Island Grows* (2006)

To demonstrate what makes good sentences, I collaborated with the science teacher across the hall to assign students this project. The author of *An Island Grows*, Lola M. Schaefer, shared this activity with me. Students do the following:

- List twelve to fifteen terms.
- Circle or check the strongest terms, usually eight to ten.
- Decide on an organizational tool—chronological order, alphabetical, steps in a process, largest to smallest, general to specific, etc.

- Order the terms.
- Add a verb to each term.
- Select three to four two-word sentences they can expand on.
- Make sidebars for in-depth explanation.

Students use the typed text as a model—short sentences with powerful verbs. Using a thesaurus as a resource to find more active verbs is a natural extension of this writing project. Derrick and Matthew wrote their imitation as a PowerPoint slide show:

> **The Water Cycle**
> *Sun shines.*
> *Water heats.*
> *Vapors rise.*
> *Clouds build.*
> *Rain falls.*
> *Lakes swell.*
> *Oceans fill.*
> *Sun shines.*
> *And the cycle goes on and on.*

Another student asked if he could write about his love: sports. I usually let my students change assignments if they come to me with an idea. Marquis came up with this:

> *A player passes.*
> *Ball flies.*
> *Girls holler.*
> *Cameras click.*
> *An agent approaches.*

This imitation experience gives students an opportunity to have fun, putting nouns and verbs together like a puzzle. A concept grows. A Georgia high school teacher I shared this activity with started using it for his students to summarize complex texts such as *Fahrenheit 451* by Ray Bradbury. Clearly, *An Island Grows* and this activity could spark a lot of learning.

5.6 Invitation to Revise

> *He started with his bookshelf. He pulled out four or five volumes from his encyclopedia and threw them on the floor. Then he tossed out a couple of comic books and a* National Geographic.
>
> *He opened every drawer in his dresser. He flipped out stuff from each one—socks, underwear, shirts. They landed all over. He kicked the waste-basket over. He dragged his dirty clothes hamper from the closet and dumped it on the floor. He charged into his desk. Pencils and papers and rubber bands went flying. About the only thing he didn't do was spit.*
>
> *By now, you could hardly see the floor. He stood in the middle, turning, nodding, smiling. "Yeah. Now it's my room."*
>
> *And he wasn't done. We ordered a pizza, and when he got down to the crust of each slice, he tossed it over his shoulder. One landed in his underwear drawer. The pizza box he flipped like a Frisbee against the wall.*
>
> —Jerry Spinelli, *Fourth Grade Rats* (1991)

This excerpt from Jerry Spinelli's book has some active verbs and at least one possibility for revision in the last sentence. I figure since the kids and I have been looking at two-word sentences, we need to expand that discussion back to their larger pieces of writing and larger sentences. Now that they see the core, they are ready for more. Of course, we usually want a variety of sentences, and only a few of our sentences will actually be two words only.

Students transfer two learnings into their writing: Sentences need subjects and verbs, and just as these two-word sentences have powerful, active verbs, so can our longer sentences.

I distribute a copy of the excerpt from *Fourth Grade Rats* to groups. I explain that this excerpt is about a kid who is too neat and perfect. He is transforming into a fourth-grade rat by messing up his room.

I get them started by putting the piece on an overhead to show them what to do.

"I think we can learn a lot from two-word sentences," I say. "What I learned as a writer is that verbs make a sentence in more than one way. Yes, you have to have one to have a sentence, but we can make our sentences even more powerful by using active verbs." I explain how we will highlight all the active verbs we see.

I model highlighting the first few verbs and then ask them to highlight the rest of the verbs and any sentences they might want to revise.

Students choose a piece of writing they want to reenter. I think it is imperative that we look back. For the first decade of my teaching career, I did a sorry job of it. I know I need to keep the kids writing daily and can't clog up writing fluency with too much reflection, but the writing is there in their portfolios and their writer's notebooks. We should return to them purposefully. And we know the sage revision advice I alluded to earlier: Put the writing in a drawer for a while and then come back to it with fresh eyes. Rereading at different points in the year ensures that they identify their strengths and weaknesses. They see what they know now, to see how they've grown. That's powerful.

Though I directed my students to look at the verbs, they found many other things they wanted to polish, even if only slightly. With me roaming around the room, stopping and sharing students' successes and questions, writing, editing, and revising happen. Making it a big conversation about our writing and what we do to make it effective is the key. That, to me, is writer's workshop—and writing process, for that matter.

5.7 *Extending* the Invitation

Getting punched hard in the face is a singular experience.
—Pete Hautman, *Godless* (2004)

Subject and verb agreement is basically all about one thing. I play the song "One" (Aimee Mann 2000) when teaching singular versus plural. One indeed is the loneliest number. We talk about how *getting punched hard in the face is a singular experience*—literally. The author didn't intend it as a grammar lesson, but it really hits home the idea that a singular experience can also be a singular subject. You can even talk about gerunds, but be careful: You might end up like Jason when he is talking to a girl he is trying to impress. His phone conversation is going flat, so he grasps for the first interesting topic that floats into his mind:

What can I say that's interesting? Perhaps an astute grammatical observation. I say, "Did you know that you start a lot of sentences with the word so*?"*

"Thanks a lot. Did you know you were an insensitive jerk?"

Hmm. Maybe she's not into grammar.
—Pete Hautman, *Godless* (2004)

6

To Be or Not to Be:
Teaching Verb Choice

INTRODUCTION

What you want students to walk away knowing about verbs:

- The verbs of being are indeed verbs.
- The verbs of being are: *is, are, was, were, be, been, am.*
- Sometimes we can avoid using a verb of being with the *-ing* form of a verb to strengthen our writing.
- Active voice can create cleaner, tighter writing.

Misunderstandings you may need to clarify:

- Confusion that verbs mean *only* actions (there are the verbs of being to contend with: *is, are, was, were, be, been, am*)
- Confusion that passive voice is the same thing as past tense

Verbs add action and movement to our writing. But the possibility of what verbs can do is so much more than that. To build this understanding, a brief explanation of verbs of being and a comparison of active and passive voice will go a long way in showing kids all that verbs can do to revise their sentences for word choice and even sentence variety. Verbs of being are important; sometimes they're exactly what we need to convey the right meaning. But often the main verb will pack a more powerful punch if it stands alone. The same goes for active voice versus passive voice. Sometimes passive voice is the right choice, but very often switching to active voice will make great improvements.

Say What?

Active Voice puts the actor or the subject of a sentence near the front of the sentence, so it can do or be. Here is a sentence in the passive voice: *Writing is weakened by the passive voice.* What weakens the writing? The passive voice. We should move the subject of the sentence up to the front: *The passive voice weakens writing.* That's the active voice.

INVITATIONS

6.1 *Invitation* to Notice

> *It was like nothing on earth we had ever seen before. Fred, Sam, and I stood in front of strange trees and giant ferns. A rocky cliff rose behind us. A volcano smoked ahead of us.*
> —Jon Scieszka, *Your Mother Was a Neanderthal* (1993)

The choices we have for verb forms may be imperceptible to many students. When teaching verb choice, my goal is to start showing kids the effects of verb choice on the power of a sentence. Young writers need a concrete way to approach editing their verbs.

I begin by reading Scieszka's original version once; then I read the weaker version I created by adding *-ing* constructions for contrast:

> *It was like nothing on earth we had ever seen before. Fred, Sam, and I were standing in front of strange trees and giant ferns. A rocky cliff was rising behind us. A volcano was smoking ahead of us.*

I ask, "What do you notice?"

Students share. Then I read both again and we discuss what they notice. We include craft in our discussion, such as beginning fiction by, as I like to say, setting up the setting—a great way to start narratives, fiction or nonfiction.

I show the two sentences to the students, highlighting the differences. Pointing to Scieszka's sentence, I say, "This version uses just the main verb, whereas the other version has verbs of being helping out the main verbs in their *-ing* form." I pause. "Which one do you think is better? Make sure you talk about why."

This would be a time to discuss that the verbs of being and the *–ing* form together show ongoing action. Sometimes kids fall into this pattern and need to see that dropping the verb of being and the *-ing* ending can add a little snap to their prose.

Groups discuss what they think and then we discuss it as a whole class.

More Mentors

> *He dashed into the house while the smell of hose water and burning plastic drifted up over the patio.*
> —Tony Abbott, *Firegirl* (2007)

To change the verbs in this sentence to the *-ing* form, we could add verbs of being: *He was dashing into the house while the smell of hose water and burning plastic was drifting up over the patio.* It sounds okay to most readers, but the writing pops when we take out the verbs of being and change the *-ing* form of the verbs.

> *Stepping out of the overheated car, Hector found himself shivering. He zipped up his flimsy nylon windbreaker and pulled the drawstring of the small hood snugly around his face, although he knew this made him look like a turtle without a shell.*
> —Lynne Rae Perkins, *Criss Cross* (2005)

Then I take it a step further. Instead of writing a sentence such as *It was cold*, a great writer can change a sentence completely by showing rather than telling. And the way we use verbs helps show more than we may realize. Lynne Rae Perkins never tells us it's cold—she never even uses the word, but we know. Note the verbs. Even when they are in the *-ing* form they aren't paired with verbs of being. They make us shiver.

Having the subject *receive the action* rather than having the subject *act* is another way to gum up the writing, this time with the passive voice. For example, Perkins writes actively: *He zipped up his flimsy nylon windbreaker.* Making the writing passive is easy. We just move the subject—sometimes referred to as the doer—to the end of the sentence to receive the action: *The flimsy nylon windbreaker was zipped by him.* Specific nouns and great verbs can become much less effective when they are used in the passive voice. This is a sophisticated fine-tuning of the writing process, yet I believe it is one way to reenter writing with a concrete way to improve it.

6.2 *Invitation* to Revise

> *Is, are, was, were, be, been, am! Is, are, was, were, be, been, am!*
> —Sarah Ryan, Burnet Junior High

I remember Ms. Ryan, my seventh-grade English teacher, chanting over and over again, "Is, are, was, were, be, been, am." We joined. We yelled. Fun was had by all. Did I say we did it over and over again? Well, that's an understatement.

Doing something of this nature familiarizes students with the verbs of being. These verbs, much maligned, are quite useful but, as with any writing tool, can be overdone. After learning the simple sentence, my students sometimes still believe verbs can mean only action, even though our sentence test asks, "What *are* they or what did they do?"

I show students the sentence from *Your Mother Was a Neanderthal* (see Figure 6.1).

Figure 6.1

CODE PASSIVE VOICE

It (was) like nothing on earth we had ever seen before. Fred, Sam, and I (were) standing in front of strange trees and giant ferns. A rocky cliff (was) rising behind us. A volcano (was) smoking ahead of us.

I draw a circle around all the "verbs of being" in the sentence, coding all occurences of *is, are, was, were, be, been, am* in the writing. Then, we work on seeing how many we can delete—at least half—from the sentence so that it still makes sense.

I take the altered version and demonstrate how it could be changed. First I review the verbs of being and then students help me identify them in the sentence. I circle each one (Carroll and Wilson 1993).

"Now that we've circled them, let's try to see how many we can delete. Our goal is to change at least half of the verbs of being. If we can't figure how to change a sentence, we move on to the next one. Sometimes verbs of being help our writing make sense."

This first sentence will more than likely stay the same, but we should give it a shot and then move on to the next sentence—a great time to emphasize again that sometimes you need verbs of being. Remember, often the verb of being is in front of an *-ing* verb. These can easily be changed, unless, of course, the writer is trying to communicate an ongoing action.

"Hey, look what you could do," I say. "What if I cut the *were* in the second sentence?" I draw a line through *were*. "Now all I have to do is change the *-ing* verb, *standing*.

"Let's see. I see that it starts with a *was*," I say, pointing back to the first sentence. "It's in the past tense, so it should be *stood*." I draw a line through *standing* and write *stood* above it, creating the new sentence: *Fred, Sam, and I stood in front of strange trees and giant ferns.*

Students help me with the next sentence: *A rocky cliff was rising behind us.* We cut the *was* and change the *-ing* verb to the past tense—irregular verbs get a moment in the sun—until we end up with *A rocky cliff rose behind us.*

Next, students turn to a partner and rewrite the final sentence, changing it to *A volcano smoked ahead of us.* We discuss how we changed it. We read it both ways, comparing and contrasting, naming which is weaker and stronger and why.

"Do you see a pattern of when it's easy to strengthen a sentence by choosing the right form of a verb?" If no one does, I show them. "Remember how each one of the verbs of being we took out was next to an *-ing* verb?"

"Oh, yeah," a few students say aloud.

Last, we compare our version with Scieszka's version.

6.3 Invitation to Combine

Ingrid Levin-Hill, three weeks past her thirteenth birthday, sat thinking in her orthodontist's waiting room.

—Peter Abrahams, *Down the Rabbit Hole* (2006)

We review yesterday's discovery about how the *-ing* verbs next to the verbs of being might be changed, and we squeeze in our verbs-of-being chant. There is another way to strengthen verbs by cutting *is, are, was, were, be, been*, and *am*. I demonstrate with the uncombined sentence from *Down the Rabbit Hole*, which makes a lot of sentences. Before I uncombine the sentences, I note the tense the sentence was originally written in. Coincidentally, the uncombined sentences are quite close to many my students write. I call them Lamaze sentences: *He, He, He, She, She, She.*

> *Ingrid Levin-Hill was thirteen.*
> *She had her birthday three weeks ago.*
> *She was sitting and thinking.*
> *She was in her orthodontist's waiting room.*

We read the sentences. "What do you notice?"

After students share, if no one has addressed it, I say, "Maybe we could combine these sentences to get rid of some of the verbs of being." First we identify what we want to delete. In this case we start with those invasive verbs of being, which we want to eradicate.

"Can we combine these sentences into one?"

"No!" Chris shouts.

I pause.

Kashmere sees me pausing and decides to yell, "Yes!" I try to remember that curing the crapshoot response takes time.

If kids are chomping at the bit, I let them try to combine them on their own. If they are not, I let them try for a few minutes; this cognitive dissonance makes them ready to listen for some tips.

I think aloud: "Okay, so Ingrid is thirteen. I bet I could mix that in. Plus, I see a verb of being next to an *-ing* verb: *was sitting*. What tense do the verbs cue me to?" We come up with this sentence:

> *Ingrid Levin-Hill, a thirteen-year-old for three weeks, sat and thought in the orthodontist's waiting room.*

We close by comparing our version with that of Peter Abrahams. Students note that neither version uses one verb of being and that combining a few sentences into one is another way to cut some of the verbs of being. Kids also discover real ways to create varying sentence patterns. Plus, the more we practice this skill, the more they will attend to lessons on sentence variety, looking for more ways to combine.

Sixth planet from the Sun, Saturn is the second largest planet; only Jupiter is larger. Named for the Roman god of agriculture, Saturn is most famous for its gleaming rings, which make the planet one of the most beautiful objects in the solar system.

> —Kenneth C. Davis, *Don't Know Much About the Universe* (2002)

The next day we look at an uncombined version of Kenneth C. Davis's sentence:

Saturn is the sixth planet from the Sun.
Saturn is the second largest planet.
Only Jupiter is larger.
It is named for the god of agriculture.
The god of agriculture is Roman.
Saturn is famous for gleaming rings.
Saturn is one of the most beautiful objects in the solar system.

Groups chip away at the sentence, arguing and testing versions. It's fun to watch my students grapple with such passion.

"No, no, it already says god of agriculture," Vidiana says. "You only have to say that once." The point isn't for them to combine the sentences into only one sentence; it's to get them thinking about options, about how we can improve our writing by combining ideas. Some come up with two or three sentences, but they are shaving it down, keeping meaning, compacting ideas. In fact, the original is in two sentences, a paragraph actually.

I roam around the room, nudging students. "Do you have to use that *is*? I'm not saying you don't—I'm just asking what you think."

After groups share the results of their combining, we talk about how and why we made the choices we did. On the overhead I show Davis's original two sentences.

6.4 *Invitation* to Write

The first Saturday in August featured perfect flea-market clouds: sun-blockers but not rain-makers. The tables on the gravel acre along Ridge Pike displayed everything from watches to monkey wrenches. One of the tables was rented by Refrigerator John, who in turn donated a third of his space to Primrose. David helped arrange the wares from their Thursday night shopping sprees. One of them was a toilet seat. A sign taped to it said, WOULDN'T THIS MAKE A CHARMING PICTURE FRAME?

> *There were also two paperback mystery novels, a painting of a bull-*
> *fighter on velvet, an old blue green Coke bottle, five baseball cards, a hub-*
> *cap, an orange-colored bowl, a vase, a beaded lizard-looking pocketbook,*
> *and under a table, the child's racing chair that John had repaired.*
>   —Jerry Spinelli, *Eggs* (2007)

After reading the passage from *Eggs* aloud, I ask students what sticks with them. I reread the passage and we list the words or phrases that stuck with us. We see, again, the power of being specific. We don't say there is a lot of stuff. We list all the things we see, reviewing the serial comma.

Students write about shopping. We brainstorm places we go to shop—the grocery store, the flea market, the mall, the convenience store, the ice cream/candy truck, wherever.

Students write and share with small groups if they like and then with the larger group—if they like.

For about three minutes, students reread their freewrites and circle all the verbs of being. Then, for about seven minutes, they try to reduce the verbs of being they have used—perhaps by half. When a student gets stuck, we write his or her sentence on the board and generate options—including one that says you probably need to leave that the way it is, and here's why. The focus is on meaning and crisp writing.

6.5 *Invitation* to Edit

> *The first Saturday in August featured perfect flea-market clouds: sun-*
> *blockers but not rain-makers. The tables on the gravel acre along Ridge*
> *Pike displayed everything from watches to monkey wrenches.*
>   —Jerry Spinelli, *Eggs* (2007)

I print a transparency with multiple versions of the mentor sentence (see Figure 6.2). I start by covering up all the sentences except the first, correct version. I ask, "What do you notice?" Next I cover up all versions except the one below the first one and ask students what has changed. We discuss the change, what effect it has, and how we could make the sentence better—usually returning it to its first version, but not necessarily.

I repeat the process, covering and uncovering, asking what students notice, the effect of the changes, and what they'd do to improve it. I sum up the learning by showing the correct version again at the end.

Figure 6.2

UNCOVERING HOW WRITERS COMMUNICATE WITH READERS

How'd They Do It?

The first Saturday in August featured perfect flea-market clouds: sun-blockers but not rain-makers. The tables on the gravel acre along Ridge Pike displayed everything from watches to monkey wrenches.
—Jerry Spinelli, *Eggs*

The first Saturday in August featured perfect flea-market clouds: sun-blockers but not rain-makers the tables on the gravel acre along Ridge Pike displayed everything from watches to monkey wrenches.

The first saturday in August featured perfect flea-market clouds: sun-blockers but not rain-makers. The tables on the gravel acre along Ridge Pike displayed everything from watches to monkey wrenches.

The first Saturday in August featured perfect flea-market clouds: sun-blockers but not rain-makers. The tables on the gravel acre along Ridge Pike display everything from watches to monkey wrenches.

The frist Saturday in August featured perfect flea-market clouds: sun-blockers but not rain-makers. The tables on the gravel acre along Ridge Pike displayed everything from watches to monkey wrenches.

After seeing the correct sentence, students identify what has changed as each subsequent sentence is uncovered separately. We are open to changes from sentence to sentence so that the activity continues to be generative.

6.6 Extending the Invitation

After lessons on verb form choice, students need to be reminded that some-times we need verbs of being and the passive voice. Perhaps we want to show an ongoing action. What if we wrote a sentence with a verb of being and *-ing* verb?

Xavier is dying.

Verbs of being can't and shouldn't be completely eradicated. If we want to build suspense or not alter the meaning, it may be more appropriate to leave the verb of being. Is it better to revise the sentence as follows?

Xavier died.
Xavier dies.

The meaning completely changes if we lose the *-ing* verb.

And how about passive voice?

My ice cream was stolen!

We can't change this to active voice. Part of the point is that the doer is unknown.

Verbs of being aren't always wrong, and neither is passive voice. We should always base our final decision on the meaning we want to communicate to a reader.

7

Let's Make It an Appositive Experience: Teaching Appositives

INTRODUCTION

What you want students to walk away knowing about appositives:

- Appositives add information to sentences by renaming nouns (people, places, or things).
- Appositives are next to the noun they are renaming.
- Appositives need commas or dashes to offset them from the sentence.

Misunderstandings you may need to clarify:

- Adding too many things to sentences and creating run-ons
- Assuming that any sentence with two commas in it contains a serial comma
- Assuming that any sentence with two commas in it contains an appositive

Appositives add information to sentences by renaming nouns—defining or summarizing them. Appositives can give students more ways to combine information and embed it in a sentence.

Say What?   **Appositive** means being positioned next to something, and this grammatical pattern is all about position. Whether punctuated with a comma or dash, an appositive should be positioned near the noun it describes.

INVITATIONS

7.1 *Invitation* to Notice

> *Catherine the Great, my Russian grandma, is already awake.*
> —Cari Best, *Three Cheers for Catherine the Great!* (2003)

"What do you notice?" I ask.

"*Great* is capitalized," says Javier.

"Why, do you think?"

"Maybe it's part of her name," adds Mercedes.

"Like she's a superhero!" blurts Patrick.

We discuss their other noticings: *Russian* is capitalized, *grandma* is not capitalized, and several students insist there is a serial comma. Though there is not, we must break it down.

"What clues do you have that it's a serial comma?"

"It's got commas like . . ."

Shaking his head, Jonathan says, "It's not a list."

"If it's not a list, it's not a serial comma." I realize this could bruise the ego, so I make sure to point out the valid reasoning they began and then take them to the next level. "Yeah, it kind of looks like a serial comma because there is more than one comma in the sentence." I walk over to the sentence. "We read to make sense of things. So let's reread the sentence: *Catherine the Great, my Russian grandma, is already awake.* There isn't a list because *my Russian grandma* just renames *whom*?"

"Catherine the Great," a few say.

"So it's not a list. And what you just said tells us something. You said the Russian grandma tells us who Catherine the Great is . . ."

"Russian! A grandma!"

I let them know we have discovered the appositive—a way to rename something or tell us more about it in one sentence. Sometimes we want to add some information about something we're writing about without writing a whole new sentence. For instance, I recently read the book *Clementine*, by Sara Pennypacker (2006). "Let's say I wanted to describe the novel's main character. I could brainstorm what I know." I write the sentences on the board as I say them.

> *Clementine is funny.*
> *She is in third grade.*
> *She lives in New York.*

"If I wanted to, I could put all of my thoughts about the main character, Clementine, in one sentence." I write the combined sentence on the board.

> *Clementine,* a funny third grader, *lives in New York.*

"So which part renames Clementine?"

If a student points out that we also cut two *verbs of being* and made the verbs more active, I will kiss the floor. If that hasn't happened yet, I will save this paper and pull it out later when we are being more explicit about the connection between appositives, combining, and active voice.

Additional Mentor Sentences for Invitations

> *Avon, a rather small snail, read a book every day.*
> —Avi, *The End of the Beginning* (2004)

> *Keith, the boy in rumpled shorts and shirt, did not know he was being watched as he entered room 215 of the Mountain View Inn.*
> —Beverly Cleary, *The Mouse and the Motorcycle* (1965)

Using the novel *Out of Patience*, I teach both the craft of the *appositive describing a place and its placement in the sentence* and *showing rather than telling*. To introduce or review these concepts, students compare a scant version of Brian Meehl's paragraph—and see that appositives can describe or rename a place.

> *She drove away.*

versus

Jake watched the red Mustang hurry down the street and turn left. Then it disappeared behind the tallest building for miles around, the abandoned grain elevator. *He listened to the squawk of the worn-out springs as the Mustang bumped over the railroad tracks, and the gun of the engine as Wanda made her break for Highway 40.*

—Brian Meehl, *Out of Patience* (2006)

Annabelle Swift, Kindergartner by Amy Schwartz

As class begins, I start by reviewing. "We have talked about renaming the noun and using commas to set off that extra naming." I hold up the picture book *Annabelle Swift, Kindergartner* (1991). "Look at the title of this book. Read the title for us, Javier."

"Annabelle Swift, Kindergartner."

Annabelle's big sister gets her ready for her first day of school and tells her a lot of things she should do—even if she shouldn't—to play a trick on her little sis. One thing she tells Annabelle to do is to introduce herself as Annabelle Swift, kindergartner. I have to read the book at this point because the students just won't let me go on till I read it.

Of course, I can't avoid stopping and writing down any appositives. There is only one besides the four times the author repeats "Annabelle Swift, kindergartner": *I'm Mr. Blum, the kindergarten teacher.*

When we discuss the examples and nonexamples we find, I ask, "What's renamed in this sentence?" For something to be renamed, it must first be named. We can see that *kindergartner* renames *Annabelle* in the title; however, in the sentence *Call your sister to dinner, Annabelle,* nothing is being renamed. In the second sentence, the comma is being used to set off a name in direct address—it doesn't rename anything.

We talk about how *kindergartner* renames *Annabelle*. It gives us another fact about her. Later, we can open up students to other ways we may embed information in our sentences with appositives, but for now we stick to the obvious renaming with nouns.

As we move into writer's workshop, I lead a mini-invitation tour: freewriting, celebrating, revising, and celebrating again. We have to pump up the good feelings, the purposeful ease of using grammar. Students freewrite about school, giving advice for the first days of the school year. Vanessa asks if she can pretend her little sister is going to middle school next year and whether she can give her advice.

"Does it have to be funny?" she asks.

"Follow your writing and see where it takes you," I say.

"Can it be funny?"

"Yes."

We take a moment afterward to reread our writing to see if we used any appositives. If students find appositives, they highlight them. If they see a place where they can add an appositive or combine sentences to create one, they highlight that as well. Students play with creating appositives. Then we share, celebrate, throw examples up on the wall—if they are renaming, we are posting. If not, we still celebrate good writing.

"Wow, that's really beautiful," I say. "It's not an appositive, and it still is fine writing." Students who are confused will be ready for the next lesson that clarifies just how we make these appositives.

7.2 *Invitation* to Combine

We combine sentences all the time. It saves time. We combine ideas in one sentence. We insert information about nouns—people, places, and things—to combine ideas. Looking back at the sentence from *Three Cheers for Catherine the Great*, I write the sentence as several sentences, showing one at a time.

Catherine the Great is awake.

"Right away, I'd wonder who Catherine the Great is. Cari Best anticipates what questions a reader would have and answers them. She could have written it this way and still answered all of our questions." I point to the sentences I've written on the board.

Catherine the Great is my grandma.
She is Russian.
She is already awake.

"But we can also combine them," I say, pointing back to the published sentence. Next students take the three sentences below and try to write them as one, combining them.

I watched her playing ladushky with Mimmo so he wouldn't cry.
Ladushky is a clapping song.
The clapping song is Russian.

Students combine sentences with a partner. We share and compare them with the published sentence:

I watched her playing ladushky, a Russian clapping song, with Mimmo so he wouldn't cry.

"Did we take out any verbs of being?"

Faces light up as they realize we have been doing double duty: creating appositives and taking out some verbs of being—which can make the voice more active rather than passive.

7.3 *Invitation* to Write

My time with Albert Einstein, my grandfather, passed all too quickly.
—Marfé Ferguson Delano, *Genius: A Photobiography of Albert Einstein* (2005)

Creating a concrete way to understand the appositive is my goal. I know if the kids use their hands, their eyes, and their minds, they are likely to remember. Appositives are quite useful for embedding information in sentences. We look at the sentence about Albert Einstein. I let kids tell me about the sentence and suppose why the writer made the choices she did.

We move right into the activity—an appositive experience. Before we start, a volunteer distributes three sheets of typing paper to each student. Making this flipbook allows students to have fun creating wacky combinations by playing the switcheroo on appositives. I borrow all the staplers I can for this activity.

To construct the booklet, I lead students step-by-step through the following process:

- Take the three sheets of white copier paper or construction paper.
- Stack all three sheets evenly.
- Fold the three sheets over in a hot-dog fold, the long way.
- Turn the paper so it's horizontal, with the folded edge at the top.
- Staple the very top on the fold three times: once near the top left, once in the middle near the crease, and once on the top right.
- Measure about three inches from each side.
- Cut all sheets from the open end at three inches from each side, almost to the top, but not quite, as the booklet will fall apart if you get too close. Leave about an eighth of an inch at the top. (See the diagram, where dashed lines represent the cutting lines.)
- On the underside of the cover, just above the stapled fold, write headings for the three flaps: *subject;*, *appositive,*; *verb:*

	[underside of cover]	
Subject	**, appositive,**	**verb**
Billybob	, an editor,	is brilliant.

After the booklet is made:

1. On the first flap, students write the subject of their first sentence. Students should write sentences on scratch paper first to make sure their sentence works.

2. On the second flap, students write an appositive—a renaming word or phrase—with a comma before and after. It can't be a whole sentence in the middle section. No section will have an entire sentence in it.

3. On the third flap, students write the main verb and the rest of the sentence to its period—the verb phrase.

4. The subjects of the sentences may be as follows:
   a. TV star
   b. Friend
   c. Rock, rap, country, or Tejano music star
   d. Car
   e. Place

Subject	**, appositive,**	**verb**
Gil Grisom	, a TV crime scene investigator,	loves insects.
Edie	, a freckle-faced mother,	drives a minivan.
Eminem	, a rap star,	released a new CD.
The Mercedes	, an expensive import,	is made in Germany.
McDonald's	, home of fat and cholesterol,	is at the end of the street.
Variety is the key, and the kids will love being clever and making funny flips. Exchanging appositives and sentence endings among rappers, TV stars, and friends will make some wacky sentences. Students rename each one and work it out on scratch paper.		

After their booklets are completed, students decorate the cover and exchange their booklets with others, flipping up different flaps to create new sentences: *McDonald's, an expensive import, released a new CD.*

7.4 Invitation to Revise

The army was led by one of Britain's most colorful officers, General John Burgoyne. Burgoyne was known as Gentleman Johnny. He was a wild character: a drinker, a gambler, actor, playwright—and a pretty good general.

    —Joy Hakim, *The History of US: From Colonies to Country, 1735–1791* (1993)

I ask a student to read the sentence about General John Burgoyne.

"Joy Hakim embedded a lot of information about General Burgoyne," I say. "What do we know about this man after reading the sentence?"

Students quietly read the sentence.

"He was one of Britain's most colorful officers," Clarissa reads aloud.

"Good, Clarissa is looking back at the sentence to answer my question. That's what I have to do to answer my own questions."

Students then name all the renaming words and phrases: *drinker, gambler, actor,* and so on.

For fun the kids uncombine the sentences. Well, not for fun really, but it could be fun. "Whoever makes the most sentences out of this will get to leave thirty seconds early."

Groups dive in and start making up new sentences on some butcher paper. When they are finished, we hang them up. We count the sentences, discuss the passive voice we have created, and again suppose why Joy Hakim made the writing decisions she made.

"She could have written this in many sentences," I say.

"Yeah, she'd be done if she'd filled up the page," Ruben smirks.

"Well, yes, I suppose she would have covered more of the page—but would she have told us anything new? That's what I wonder."

Captain Nathan Hale was a 21-year-old schoolteacher just out of Yale College when he accepted a dangerous mission.

    —Joy Hakim, *The History of US: From Colonies to Country, 1735–1791* (1993)

The next day I showed them another sentence from Joy Hakim's book. "What do you notice?"

Dead silence.

"Well, I think we could change it with what we've been learning." I circle the *was* and ask, "What if we took that out?"

We collaborate to create this new version of the sentence:

Captain Nathan Hale, a 21-year-old schoolteacher just out of Yale College, accepted a dangerous mission.

We've made the verbs more active and cut three words out. Not bad. But now we have to explore whether the new sentence is better—and it's all a matter of opinion.

7.5 *Invitation* to Edit

Frank's house looked like it had been drawn by a kindergartner with only two crayons, lime green and sunflower.
—Paul Acampora, *Defining Dulcie* (2006)

I show the sentence from *Defining Dulcie* and ask what they notice. After our discussion, I cover the original sentence and show another version of it where one thing was changed (see Figure 7.1). Students identify the change, compare the effect of the change, and decide which version they like better.

As the lesson comes to a close, I ask what Paul Acampora taught us about writing with his sentence.

"He used description."

"How'd Acampora do that?"

"He used a simile," Vanessa says.

I ask her to read the simile.

"It looked like it was drawn by a kindergartner."

Students laugh.

I ask, "What else?"

"He names the colors' names, but not like green and yellow. He's says lime and sunflowers," Luis says.

"Yeah, I like that too," I say. We discuss the apostrophes and anything else students think we could do as writers.

Then I ask students to try something they learned today in their own writing. I ask them to make sure to share their successes with the class. I keep my

Figure 7.1

UNCOVERING HOW WRITERS COMMUNICATE WITH READERS

How'd They Do It?

Frank's house looked like it had been drawn by a kindergartner with only two crayons, lime green and sunflower.
—Paul Acampora, *Defining Dulcie* (2006)

Franks house looked like it had been drawn by a kindergartner with only two crayons, lime green and sunflower.

Frank's house looks like it was drawn by a kindergartner with only two crayons, lime green and sunflower.

Frank's house looked like it had been drawn by a kindergartner with only two crayons, lime green and sunflower.

Frank's house looked like it had been drawed by a kindergartner with only two crayons, lime green and sunflower.

Frank's house looked like it had been drawn by a kindergartner with only two Crayons, lime green and sunflower.

After the correct sentence is shown, students identify changes as each subsequent sentence is uncovered separately. We are open to changes from sentence to sentence so that the activity continues to be generative.

---

eyes open, and when I see a student using some of the craft we focused on today, I ask him or her to share it in print or aloud.

7.6 *Extending* the Invitation

It should be noted that appositives can be more than simply nouns that rename the noun close by. Appositives are made of description—attributes, details, and comparisons (Christensen and Christensen 1976). In short an appositive can do more than simply rename a person. The description it provides sharpens the image, amplifying it with new information and clarifying the meaning for the reader. First, the appositive pattern becomes imprinted in its simplest form: *Ty, a defensive back, was only a few yards from her.* Abrahams, a skilled writer, uses many appositives to make his meaning clear. Once that pattern is established, it is easy for writers to go beyond simple renaming to a more sophisticated strategy that adds clarity and beauty to writing.

> *It was twilight, that time of day when shadows grow long and the lights starts to fade and a dog's eyes can play tricks on her.*
> —Ann M. Martin, *A Dog's Life* (2005a)

> *Joey was in their grade, a big pudgy kid with a cowlick that stood up at the back of his head like a blunt Indian feather.*
> —Peter Abrahams, *Down the Rabbit Hole* (2006)

> *Ingrid panned the beam across the room, a furnace room full of shadows, cobwebs, newspaper stacks, junk.*
> —Peter Abrahams, *Down the Rabbit Hole* (2006)

Give Me a Break: Teaching Paragraphs

INTRODUCTION

What you want students to walk away knowing about paragraphs:

- Paragraphs have a purpose.
- Paragraphs help readers and writers chunk information together and separate it as well.
- Paragraphs may have any number of sentences. There is no rule.
- Paragraphs help the reader understand writing.
- Paragraphs tend to focus on one main idea (unity), and its parts should be related (coherence).

Misunderstandings you may need to clarify:

- The belief that because paragraphs have a purpose, they have to be hard
- Thinking that paragraphs have to follow a formula
- Subscribing to the idea that all paragraphs should be five sentences long

In "Whatever Happened to the Paragraph?" Mike Duncan (2007) says, "Hold a typed page ten feet away—the words fade into smudges, but the indented visual structure remains." Considered punctuation by many, this one convention will stir quite a controversy. Duncan sums up the history of paragraph theory. The traditional or prescriptivist view prescribes, among other things, topic sentences and a sequential arrangement (Bain 1866). (Bain's approach was called "old school" in a 1922 issue of the *English Journal*.) Other scholars argued as early as the 1890s that the topic sentence should be "freed from mandatory positional constraints." In an NCTE symposium on the paragraph in 1966, a frustrated A. L. Becker concluded: "Paragraphs are units that the writer, for one reason or another, chooses to mark as paragraphs. This is the only way to describe all paragraphs" (Duncan 2007). I found Isaac Babel's quote in *Reading Like a Writer* more inspiring: "A new paragraph is a wonderful thing. It lets you quietly change the rhythm, and it can be a flash of lightning that shows the same landscape from a different aspect" (Prose 2006).

Say What?

Pilcrow. That's what I said: pilcrow. That's what you call that little backward *P* that means "new paragraph": ¶ = pilcrow. Though I could find no empirical proof for this, some say that the pilcrow came about through changes in how texts are made. Recall the illumination, a monk's ornate decoration of the first letter of a sentence. When the printing press came along, they needed to mark a spot for the illumination to be drawn later. Eventually, the illumination gave way to that first letter becoming larger, as you periodically see in modern texts (see page 1 of this book, for instance), and the space was then reduced to indentation. It's such a fun explanation; I hope it's true.

INVITATIONS

8.1 *Invitation* to Notice

Do you know what it's like to be in a room full of people, but to feel completely alone? Outside of the noise and all of the talking and the eating—just apart from it all? That's how I felt tonight in the Rosarios' kitchen.

I've known the Rosario family since I was a little baby. I've been over to their house a million times. But tonight it was like noticing it all for the first time. Noticing not just what everything looked like, but how it all felt. When I stopped to think about it, I realized how happy it all made me—these same things, the same people, that I have seen over and over again, my whole life long.

The Rosarios' kitchen is bright yellow. The wall by the stove is stained brown with oil splatters from the stove. It's one of those kitchens that's like a magnet; whenever friends come over, everyone ends up in the kitchen. There is a long wooden counter where Magda was sitting on a tall stool, next to the carimanolas. My mother was rolling the meat into butter and handing it over to Tia Lusia. The two of them were yacking away in Spanish; their hands flying as fast as their words.

> —Veronica Chambers, *Marisol and Magdalena: The Sound of Our Sisterhood* (1998)

Before class I typed the *Marisol and Magdalena* passage without paragraph indentions, making it one block of text. I distribute half-sheet copies of the altered passage to groups. Together, we read the passage. "What do you notice?"

After students exhaust their personal noticings, Joshua says, "That's a long paragraph."

"Yeah, it is. I have to admit something," I say. "When I typed this passage, I left off the indentions for the paragraphs."

"I suppose we have to put them back," Ernesto says, shaking his head side to side.

I write some directions on the overhead (see Figure 8.1). Students reread the passage and figure out the best place to divide up the passage into paragraphs. This is the perfect time to teach the time-saving editing mark, the pilcrow.

Figure 8.1

DISCOVERING PARAGRAPH STRUCTURE

I Will Divide!

1. Reread the passage.
2. Discuss how and why your group will divide the passage into paragraphs.
3. Use the paragraph symbol ¶ to indicate where your group would start each paragraph.

Figure 8.2

PARAGRAPH CHART

What we know about paragraphs:

- Paragraphs aren't always five sentences long.
- *Para* means "beside." *Graph* means "mark."
- ¶ = Indent new paragraph here.
- Indenting paragraphs
  —gives readers a break;
  —shows when one thought ends and another begins;
  —helps writers connect and organize thoughts.

Students share their divisions, and we compare and contrast the different responses and reasoning. We conclude that paragraphs

- show readers how information is chunked and connected;
- indicate to readers when a new idea is coming;
- are open to interpretation.

Over time, we keep collecting our thinking about principles of paragraphing on chart paper (Figure 8.2).

8.2 *Invitation* to Notice

After the discussion resulting from Invitation 8.1, I realize many of my students believe paragraphs are always five sentences long. I discuss this problem with my friend Mark Overmeyer, an educator and writer. He once used a newspaper to demonstrate that paragraphs don't always have five sentences. I knew I could do something with that pile of newspapers!

In class the next day, I give groups one newspaper and the "Down for the Count" handout (Figure 8.3). Groups do the following:

- Select a newspaper article.
- Read the article.
- Return to the first ten paragraphs of the article.

Figure 8.3

DOWN FOR THE COUNT!

Title of Written Work:

Author:

Genre:

Paragraph Number	Number of Sentences in Paragraph	Read the section of the written work and then answer these questions:
		• How do the paragraph breaks affect the reader? • How do you think the writer chose where to put the paragraph breaks? • Does this follow the rules you have been taught?

This chart can be used for any genre to see how paragraph patterns vary from genre to genre, text to text.

- Mark the number of each paragraph on the left-hand column.
- Record the number of sentences each paragraph contains on the right-hand column of the chart.

I give each group ten sticky notes. They write the number of sentences they counted in each of the ten paragraphs from the newspaper, or the right-hand column, on the sticky note. For example, Dora's group lays out all their sticky notes on the desk. They look at the first paragraph for which they counted sentences. The first paragraph had two sentences, so they write 2 on the sticky note. Next, they look at the second paragraph. This paragraph had three sentences, so they record a 3 on that sticky note to represent that they had a paragraph with three sentences. The group continues to go paragraph by paragraph, writing only the number of sentences in each of the ten paragraphs on each sticky note.

On the board I create a chart (see Figure 8.4) to make a bar graph for the students to see the paragraph trends.

Figure 8.4

HOW MANY SENTENCES DOES A PARAGRAPH HAVE?							
1 Sentence	2 Sentences	3 Sentences	4 Sentences	5 Sentences	6 Sentences	7 Sentences	8 or More Sentences

I create a chart that students affix their sticky notes to. Each sticky note will represent the number of sentences in each paragraph. Since we are creating a bar graph, students start attaching the sticky notes at the bottom line of the chart so each sticky note truly represents a unit.

After groups write the sentence count on each of their sticky notes, a group member goes to the board and places each sticky note beneath the sentence headings. Dora's group places four sticky notes under the *1 Sentence* heading on the chart because they found that four out of their ten paragraphs were made up of one sentence. Remind students to begin placing sticky notes on the bottom of the chart and to place each subsequent sticky note above the last. I really have to monitor this.

My students are surprised to see that the five-sentence paragraph column has only two sticky notes, whereas the one-, two-, and three-sentence paragraph columns have the most sticky notes. Students return to answer the questions. Afterward, we discuss their responses.

Dora's group shares that their former teacher had told them paragraphs must have four to five sentences. We discuss the implications of what we found in the newspapers today. I close the discussion by asking some questions: "Do you think that we'd get the same results if we did this with our novels? Textbooks? How do paragraphs serve the reader and the writer? How do we decide when to make a new paragraph?"

Figure 8.5 offers some important points about paragraphs.

Figure 8.5

WHAT IS A PARAGRAPH?

In *Acts of Teaching* (1993), Carroll and Wilson remind us of some key points about paragraphs. I summarize them here:

- "To indent is to interpret" (Rodgers 1966).
- Paragraphs follow "a chain of thought" rather than a rote formula.
- It's dangerous to teach students a paragraph formula rather than a paragraph strategy.
- Sometimes writers start with a topic sentence and sometimes they don't.
- Don't teach something about paragraphing that real writers don't do.

8.3 Invitation to Write

You don't know me.

Just for example, you think I'm upstairs in my room doing my homework. Wrong. I'm not in my room. I'm not doing my homework. And even if I were up in my room I wouldn't be doing my homework, so you'd still be wrong. And it's really not my room. It's your room because it's in your house. I just happen to live there right now. And it's really not my homework because my math teacher, Mrs. Moonface, assigned it and she's going to check it, so it's her homework.

Her name's not Mrs. Moonface, by the way. It's really Mrs. Garlic Breath. No it's not. It's really Mrs. Gabriel, but I just call her Mrs. Garlic Breath, except for the times when I call her Mrs. Moonface.

Confused? Deal with it.

You don't know me at all. You don't know the first thing about me. You don't know where I am writing this from. You don't know what I look like. You don't have power over me.

What do you think I look like? Skinny? Freckles? Wire-rimmed glasses over brown eyes? No, I don't think so. Better look again. Deeper. It's like a kaleidoscope, isn't it? One minute I'm geeky, one minute studly, my shape constantly changes, and the only thing that stays constant is my brown eyes. Watching you.

—David Klass, *You Don't Know Me* (2002)

We begin the class by reviewing the paragraph chart (Figure 8.1). If reviewing the chart is becoming rote, I shake it up and cover the chart. In groups, students brainstorm what they remember about the chart or paragraphs in general—even making a new point. As long as it's about paragraphing, it's game. Remember, brainstorming is writing—I forget that sometimes. The team with the best list leaves class one minute early.

After the brainstorming winners have been chosen, I tell everybody to take a breath as a transition, and then I read the *You Don't Know Me* passage twice. Students write, starting with the sentence *You don't know me.* I remind them to use what they know about paragraphs to chunk their writing. To get honest writing, I promise students they won't have to share their writing, though they may want to. Adolescents enjoy sharing what they think no one sees or understands about them.

After students write, volunteers share. Then we do a quick reread at the end of class or the beginning of class the next day, checking our paragraphing.

8.4 *Invitation* to Revise

What Is Character?

Champions have, among other things, the courage to believe in their dreams, the desire to make their dreams a reality, the integrity to do what is right, the cognitive ability to know the details of the game, the resilience to keep getting up, the determination to not give in, and the self-discipline to do what is necessary. This list can be summed up by one word—character. Character includes what a player is made of, how he performs in challenging circumstances, and how he acts when everything goes against him. These elements may be just as important as, or even more important than raw talent. Players may be chock full of physical ability, but character is what separates the wheat from the chaff.

One young quarterback, coming out of the University of Notre Dame, was deemed slow on his feet, with only an average arm. That young quarterback of supposedly average talent led the San Francisco 49ers to four Super Bowl victories. Joe Montana had instinct. Desire. Poise. Cognitive ability. He had character.

—Jim Murphy, *Dugout Wisdom: The Ten Principles of Championship Teams* (2003a)

We review the paragraph chart (Figure 8.1), adding anything else we have noticed. I make a transparency of the paragraphs from *Dugout Wisdom*, and we read them aloud.

"What do you notice?"

"It's about football," José Luis comments.

"What else?"

"It's not just about football," Vanessa adds.

"What do you mean?"

We continue our discussion about how the paragraphs are about character. In fact, the subheading signals us: *What Is Character?* The first paragraph paints the big picture of what character is, a defining paragraph, which is followed by a specific example of how character bolstered a specific player's career. We look not only at the chunks but at how each chunk is connected with the other paragraph.

Afterward, students choose a piece of writing, or I direct them to a draft to look again at their paragraphs, focusing more and more on content. Students reread their writing and then write a quick reflection on how they make paragraphs and how they will make paragraphs more effectively. We share our reflections.

Later, I follow up with other ways paragraphs may be constructed. Sometimes physical descriptions are more appropriate. We can move our writer's eye around like a camera, too, as we do in narratives. As an example, I share a paragraph from *Acceleration*:

> *Here's the one-minute tour of the place. First, to get here you have to come to the Bay subway station and take the service elevator down to the sub-basement. At the end of the hall to your left you'll find the door marked* LOST AND FOUND. *Jacob, my supervisor, sits at the front counter cataloguing the lost junk that comes in from the buses and subways in the transit system. If you think of a half-deflated soccer ball with two of the hairiest ears you've ever seen attached to it, you've got a picture of Jacob. Past the counter there's a maze of stacks holding row after row after row, shelf after dusty shelf of stuff.*
> —Graham McNamee, *Acceleration* (2003)

8.5 Invitation to Edit

I type a few passages of several paragraphs without paragraph divisions as I did for *Marisol and Magdelena*. I call this activity "Paragraphs Without Borders," an extension of "I Will Divide" (Invitation 8.1).

For a change, I create stations around the room. Stations in my middle school classroom are several little clusters of four desks shoved together. At each station, I place a stack of passages from which I removed the paragraphing. Groups each start at one station, following this procedure:

1. Read the passage.
2. Reread the passage.
3. Mark spots where paragraphs should begin with the new-paragraph symbol ¶.
4. Sign names at the bottom of the paragraph.
5. Compare and contrast with the published text.
6. Place editing work in "The Proof Is in the Paragraph" file at the station.
7. Move to the next station.
8. Repeat 1–6 with a new passage.

I make transparencies of a few of the paragraph markings that groups made. Over the next few days, we compare our different approaches to the paragraphing.

8.6 Extending the Invitation

Whenever I can, I directly connect reading-comprehension strategies with writing strategies. For instance, I teach a summary strategy called Most Important Word (Bleich 1975). Students select the most important word to describe a passage. The word can be in the passage or can be another word or two that represent the reading.

Students also do this paragraph by paragraph to understand longer texts. I realized, quite accidentally, that the most important word strategy also benefits students in understanding that each paragraph has a focus, and that when the focus changes, a new paragraph begins. Students combine what they know from comprehension instruction, making the connection that writers help readers understand when a paragraph has a main focus.

Then students take the most important word strategy back into their own writing. They select a text they have written and try to label the most important word next to each of their paragraphs. If students struggle to find a one-word focus, they may need to revise.

9

Do We Have Chemistry? Teaching Compound Sentences

INTRODUCTION

What you want students to walk away knowing about compound sentences:

- Compound sentences are made when two or more sentences are combined with a comma and a coordinating conjunction.
- Coordinating conjunctions can be remembered with the mnemonic FAN-BOYS—*for, and, nor, but, or, yet, so.*
- Compound sentences can be represented in a formula: Sentence + **,** + one of the FANBOYS + sentence + **.** = Compound Sentence.

Misunderstandings you may need to clarify:

- Confusion that any sentence with one of the FANBOYS is a compound sentence
- Confusion that any sentence with one comma is a compound sentence
- Confusion that compound sentences can't be combined with any other sentence form

Say What?

Compound. In chemistry class, we learned that a compound is something made by combining two or more different things. It's the same with compound sentences. Though we define the compound sentence pattern as joining two sentences with a comma and one of the FANBOYS, we can combine three—or perhaps more—sentences with commas and FANBOYS.

Compound sentences can also be formed by joining two related sentences with a semicolon. (That's right. No need for the FANBOYS. The semicolon joins alone.) *The separation is more subtle; sometimes we want less separation between sentences.* And, like chemistry, how and what you combine have neutral, wonderful, or disastrous results.

INVITATIONS

9.1 *Invitation* to Notice

Nick Allen had plenty of ideas, and he knew what to do with them.
—Andrew Clements, *Frindle* (1998)

To begin, I slap a compound sentence on the overhead: *Nick Allen had plenty of ideas, and he knew what to do with them.* This sentence is from a craft-filled chapter in *Frindle* from the compound-using author Andrew Clements.

And it's simple. To introduce something as mind-boggling as the compound sentence to eleven-year-olds, you better keep it simple.

"What do you notice about this sentence?" I ask.

"It's kind of funny," Julian replies.

"I agree, Julian. Why do you think that is?"

Biting his lip and looking at the sentence, he finally says, "You agreed with me, so why don't you tell us why it's funny?"

Touché. "I want your help to think about it, that's why I am asking."

Samantha chimes in, "Well, it makes you think maybe the ideas he gets aren't so good, but he does 'em anyway."

"Yeah, what she said," Julian says.

The class laughs.

Laughing too, I say, "I hadn't thought about it that way, Samantha. I like it."

I look around the room. "What else do you notice?"

I make sure to give plenty of wait time for answers. Student responses are more complex when they have about ten seconds to think. I resist the urge to interrupt the silence and tell the kids "the answer."

"I wonder what his ideas are."

As I listen to their responses, I repeat the invitation. "What else do you notice?" waiting, listening, commenting, questioning, and returning. "What else?"

"You know what I notice. This looks like two sentences in one." I model some targeted thinking I want the kids to see or hear, but only if I first invited and gave kids multiple opportunities to notice. Once the concept is modeled, if necessary, kids tune in to other aspects of sentences.

I point to the first half of the sentence: *Nick Allen had plenty of ideas.* "Let's give it a pop sentence test: Who or what did or is something?"

"Nick."

"Right. What did Nick do?" I ask.

"He had plenty of ideas."

I draw squiggly explosion marks around the verb *had.*

"Nice! He had a lot of ideas. So is that a sentence all by itself?"

"Yes."

I write the word *sentence* on the board and draw a box around it (see Figure 9.1). "How'd you know?"

After we think through how they knew it was a sentence, I say, "But look, there's another sentence on the other side too. Let's do the test again. What's the question we ask to find the subject?"

"Who or what did or is something?"

"And that's?"

"He . . . I mean Nick."

Drawing a line under *he,* I say, "Exact-a-mundo." Turning back to the class, "What's the question I ask to find the verb?" I can sneak in simple sentence review without stepping it back to teaching parts of speech. We can review it in the context of discovering compound sentences.

"What did he do or what is he?" They answer their own question: "He knew."

"Right, *he knew.* So this is a sentence too." I add to my pattern and pause. "Does the second sentence start with a capital letter?"

"No."

Thinking aloud, I say, "Hmm, so I won't capitalize the second *sentence*? Okay, but how did they stick these two sentences together?"

"A comma."

Figure 9.1

BUILDING THE COMPOUND SENTENCE PATTERN

| **Sentence** | , | for
and
nor
but
or
yet
so | **sentence** | . |

Nick Allen had plenty of ideas, and he knew what do to with them.

To help illustrate the pattern of the compound sentence, I draw a representation of a basic compound sentence pattern based on a graphic found in *Acts of Teaching* (Carroll and Wilson 1993). I intentionally use the terms *sentence* rather than *independent clause* and *FANBOYS* rather than *coordinating conjunctions* to simplify the pattern. To build concepts, students need to begin as simply as possible, building the pattern and its exceptions over time.

"And what else?" I say, pointing to the *and* if necessary.

"*And.*"

"So, the author stuck two sentences together instead of separating them with a period. He joined them with . . ." I wait for the answer. The kids should have some of the answers. What would I communicate about editing if only I gave the answers?

"A *comma*—and an *and.*"

I fill in the *comma* and the *and* on the chart.

I go back over the original sentence, connecting its components back to the pattern we are building on the chart: sentences on each side, joined with a comma, followed by an *and*. "What am I missing?"

"The period."

I add the period, ending up with a final visual pattern to begin our understanding (Figure 9.1).

I add the sentence we looked at on the chart paper below the visual pattern of the compound sentence we just created. This chart will serve as a scaffold on which we attach our future learnings about compound sentences. If we come across a compound sentence, we discuss it, especially if it uses another of the joiners or coordinating conjunctions—*for, and, nor, but, or, yet, so*. But I also intentionally add new compound sentences into the mix.

Students begin to notice and see the puzzle pieces that make up compound sentences. This invitation to notice is the place to begin with any editing concept or pattern: What does this look like? What is good about the sentence besides the punctuation and grammar patterns? What does this pattern do? How do writers do it?

> *I think about going in my room now, but it smells like the inside of an old lunch bag in there.*
> —Gennifer Choldenko, *Al Capone Does My Shirts* (2004)

To continue teaching the compound sentence, I keep giving students things to notice. I know from my years of teaching that it takes time for kids to get the concept of the compound sentence. They need many more examples. I also know that an immersion in the compound sentence over time makes owning the concept an attainable goal for them.

We've written about rooms and smells before. That's good. I want everything nice and familiar so that kids can see the underlying pattern. I put the sentence from *Al Capone Does My Shirts* on the board.

"What do you notice?" I ask.

"Mr. Anderson!" Miranda says. "Why do you have to start my day with things that smell?"

"Well, it seems to pep you up. What else do you notice?"

"It has a simile?"

"Read that for us." And we discuss the simile, the sensory detail.

We give the sentence the sentence test. It's a great time to review what it takes to make a sentence.

"Who or what did or is something?" Jessica reads off the wall.

"Well?" I ask the class.

We settle on *I* for now.

"What are they or what did they do?" Jonathan is reading from the chart we made on the wall, but he is acting like he isn't.

We can easily see that *think* is the verb and *I* is the subject. I then ask students to turn to a partner and together go through the process of deciding whether there is a complete second sentence. They ask the sentence questions that Jessica and Jonathan reminded us of. We establish that there are two sentences. "What are the two sentences attached with?"

Silence.

Basically, they don't want to feel stupid, so I just provide more help. I point to the two things that are connecting the sentences, maybe even jump up and down a little—whatever it takes.

Over the next several days—often at the beginning of class, but not always—we continue to look at and discuss how authors craft compound sentences. I can use the following sentences or ones the students and I encounter in our reading.

More Mentor Sentences

He tried to stare into her fiery gaze, but he couldn't stop looking at the purple vein bulging in her forehead.
    —Brian Meehl, *Out of Patience* (2006)

Rowanne had slipped away from her roly-poly childhood like a sylph from a cocoon, but Hector's was still wrapped around him in a soft, wooly layer.
    —Lynne Rae Perkins, *Criss Cross* (2005)

The dark scares us, for we don't know what is waiting in the dark.
    —Alvin Schwartz, *Scary Stories 3: More Tales to Chill Your Bones* (2001)

I could remember every detail of the whole night, but it had the unreal quality of a dream.
    —S. E. Hinton, *The Outsiders* (1997)

He flails and tries to swim away, but the current is too powerful.
    —Cecelia Tishy, *All in One Piece* (2007)

Angeline would reveal no secrets now, and Damiana would reveal no secrets later.
    —Sharon Shinn, *The Safe-Keeper's Secret* (2004)

Pee Wee tried to push against Melissa, but she was rooted to the floor.
    —Polly Horvath, *The Trolls* (2001)

Mom says finishing everything on his own plate is one thing, but Dad usually finishes everything on everyone else's plates, too.
    —Sarah Littman, *Confessions of a Closet Catholic* (2005)

As an outgrowth of our noticings, I introduce my students to the coordinating conjunctions. "Do you see the compound sentences? Let's break them down." After discussing how there is both a subject and a verb on both sides of the first sentence, I match it to the visual pattern (Figure 9.1) and show them how it connects. "What's new?"

Ebony discovers that the two sentences are joined by a comma followed by *but* this time—a perfect time to introduce all the coordinating conjunctions. If I say we're going to learn about coordinating conjunctions, all the air is sucked out of the room and their eyes glaze over. So I say, "There are a couple more words that connect compound sentences" and I show them the cartoon versions of the FANBOYS (see Figure 9.2).

"Do you know the FANBOYS?"

"Who?"

"You already know two of them."

"Huh?"

"You can use all the FANBOYS to join two sentences." I point out the rest of the coordinating conjunctions and we chant them. Then we orally try to

Figure 9.2

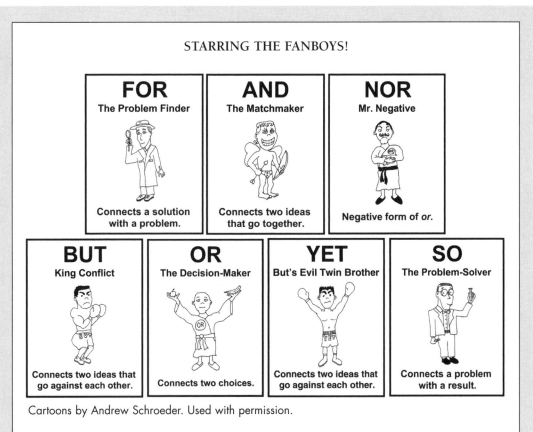

Cartoons by Andrew Schroeder. Used with permission.

imitate the pattern, reviewing the visual pattern (Figure 9.1) and adding our new learning to it. I get them started. I say, "I knew how to write a sentence, but now I know how to write longer sentences."

We talk in compound sentences for a while, trying to use as many of the FANBOYS as we can, checking to make sure we have a subject and verb on each side. We say the word *comma* to practice its placement. For clarity in these examples, I printed the comma, but we say *comma* when reciting our compound sentences.

I kick off "compound sentence talking" with "The students listen well, and Mr. Anderson lets them go to lunch early." I ask, "Do you hear two sentences?"

"Yeah."

I repeat the sentence and then ask, "What's the first sentence?"

Abigail describes it, and then I ask for the second sentence, sometimes needing to repeat the whole sentence. Last I ask, "How did I join the two sentences?" Then I challenge students to talk in compound sentences. If I am not hearing any, I say, "We want to leave early for lunchtime, but we're not sharing enough compound sentences."

Groans.

Ruben raises his hand with Eddie Haskell sincerity. "Mr. Anderson is nice, so he will let us go early," punctuating his sentence with a raised eyebrow, head tilted to the side, nodding his head up and down.

I ask what each sentence is and how they are joined. This goes on for a while. Finally, Ruben chimes in, "Everybody is talking in compound sentences, and I am getting sick."

Of course I ask, "What's the first sentence in Ruben's compound sentence?"

9.2 *Invitation* to Imitate

It's Friday night, and Mom is yelling at me because I won't eat the chicken she cooked for dinner.
　　—Sarah Littman, *Confessions of a Closet Catholic* (2005)

I sat near the back with Stephen, and he kept pestering me.

Stephen is my best friend, but I'm not sure he'd admit it.

There was only about a block to go before our bus stop, but I couldn't stand Stephen's whining another second.
　　—Andrew Clements, *The Report Card* (2004)

Over the next week or so, we look at several compound sentences, alternating the different coordinating conjunctions or FANBOYS—*for, and, nor, but, or, yet, so*—to build familiarity with the patterns and meanings. The most-used coordinating conjunctions—*and, but, or*—make up only one-third of the FANBOYS. You will notice in your reading that you rarely stumble upon *for* and *nor*, although you will see a *yet* joining a compound sentence every now and then.

The kids are ready to try an imitation.

The next day I put a few sentences on the overhead. We read them and I tell students we are going to imitate them. We review how to imitate sentences—matching pattern, not content.

I choose to imitate Littman's first sentence: *It's Friday night, and Mom is yelling at me because I won't eat the chicken she cooked for dinner.* I share my imitation: It's Sunday night, and my mom is eating Colby cheese and watching *Murder, She Wrote.*

"Now, that sentence is true, but you can also make one up. We're going for the pattern here—two related sentences joined with a comma and one of the FANBOYS." For my made-up imitation, I used Clements's sentence. My imitation follows.

> *There was only about a block to go before our bus stop, but I couldn't stand Stephen's whining another second.*

> *It was only one mile until we reached the rest stop, but I couldn't hold it for another second.*

Students find one they like and imitate it in as many ways as they can or choose several to imitate. Patrick is dying to share his imitation:

> *Andrew wants to be my best friend, but I'm not going to let him.*

Did I say that you better warn your students not to make fun of anyone at school, and to use other names for people when saying something that is not complimentary? Luckily, Patrick and Andrew really are best friends.

Vanessa shares her imitation:

> *It's Friday night, and my mom works all night. I stay up and watch scary movies, so I won't be bored. I think this plan will work, but it never does.*

"Hold on! I think we just heard three compound sentences in a row!" I say, falling into a nearby chair. "I think it's a beautiful sentence miracle, so we should all take a moment of silence to honor all that is compound."

9.3   Invitation to Write

I found several wonderful stories in *Guys Write for Guys Read,* edited by Jon Scieszka (2005). In the story "Let's Go to the Videotape," Dan Gutman reflects on his continued lack of athletic prowess throughout his lifetime, but he always remembers one moment of athletic perfection—like a videotaped memory that he can play anytime in his mind. Before the compound-sentence collecting, I read aloud the short story.

Afterward, students, like Gutman, write about a time they did something impressive or about experiences in gym in general, past or present. It's like the lunchroom: Gym class is great material for writing.

This invitation to write works in two ways: We know students get better at writing by writing. Writing is a great place to try out compound sentences. Students need many opportunities to apply patterns, first in small starts, like imitations, then moving into a writer's notebook entry or freewrite, and finally into larger writing pieces of writing such as essays and narratives.

9.4   Invitation to Collect

But usually, the game we played in gym was kickball. I liked kickball, mostly because nobody had to take off his shirt to play it.

There were about a dozen boys on each team, and the fielders would scatter across the big gym. Little guys like me would try to hit dribblers past the infield and scoot to first base before the ball got there. Big guys could bang the ball as far as they could and bounce it off the far wall.

—Dan Gutman, "Let's Go to the Videotape," found in *Guys Write for Guys Read* (2005)

I want my kids to test their budding knowledge of compound sentences in a larger text, so they don't just get the idea that they should compound-up all their sentences. At the same time, I don't just want to let students loose in books to find compound sentences. It's a little too messy to start with. It's one thing to find one and share it; it's another for me to direct everyone to find one. So I chose a short story, "Let's Go to the Videotape" by Dan Gutman, because it's of high interest and is a great spark for writing ideas, but most of all because it is chock full of simple, clean compound sentences. If this book is not available, the first chapter of *Frindle* by Andrew Clements will work as well.

The next day, I distribute the short story to groups of three or four. We review our visual scaffold we created on chart paper (see Figure 9.1) and some examples of compound sentences. It is crucial to review how to decide whether a sentence is compound or not. At first, students often think that any sentence with an *and* in it needs a comma or is a compound. Look, they say, I wrote a compound sentence: *I love to eat cheese, and fish.* This is when we take a deep breath and remember that this error will lead the child to understanding. They are overgeneralizing that the *and* alone makes a compound sentence. They just need to be talked through the compound sentence test:

- Are there two complete sentences, with subjects and verbs on each side of the FANBOYS?
- Are a comma and one of the FANBOYS joining the two complete sentences?
- Does the sentence meet *all* the criteria?

As I circulate and field questions with groups, I model the thought process for determining if a sentence is compound or not through these questions. Then, in groups, kids discuss the thought process among themselves: testing their own concept development and making sense of the pattern and its meaning. Each group gets a transparency and an overhead marker. They record all the sentences they think are compound sentences, putting them to the test. They will ask about sentences that start with *but*. Do you connect it to the sentence before? They think there has to be one on the first page, but there isn't. After most students have completed recording their compound sentences, groups present at the overhead, proving with the compound-sentence test why each of their sentences is indeed a compound one.

Ebony's group comes up to the front of the class and shares this sentence: *Baseball was always my favorite sport, but I couldn't hit the ball.*

"Okay, did anyone else include that sentence? Prove that it's a compound sentence." If they can't, I ask questions. "Does each side of the compound sentence have a subject and verb? Prove it. How are the two complete sentences joined?" To wake everybody up, I say, "Stand up if you think this is a compound sentence."

The class stands. "Check this sentence off on your transparency." As each group presents, we see a series of compounds:

> *There were about a dozen boys on each team, and the fielders would scatter across the big gym.*

> *I looked down the line, and Edmund was right.*

Then we can have some great discussions about sentences such as *It was my turn to kick and I was mad* and we suppose why the author didn't choose to use a comma to separate the two sentences. Is it so it will read faster, without the pause a comma would cause? Is it because the sentences are both so short? They're thinking—about meaning. Other poser compound sentences sneak in:

> *It looked like it had a chance to reach the far wall, or at least the basketball backboard that was attached to the wall.*

If you close your eyes and listen to the second half of the second sentence joined with *or*, can you hear that it doesn't stand on its own? But it still follows that compound pattern, doesn't it? We are talking about patterns, making sense, and the effects of our editing choices.

9.5 *Invitation* to Combine

To invite kids into combining, I uncombine some sentences and students recombine them. For example, I separate compound sentences from Nancy Osa's book *Cuba 15* (2003) and ask kids how they'd combine them. I write the uncombined sentences on the board.

> *A nervous chuckle rose up in me.*
> *I refused to let it out.*

> *I tried calling her as soon as I got home from school.*
> *Her line was busy.*
>   —Nancy Osa, *Cuba 15* (2003)

Students combine the sentence pairs and create two compound sentences in their writer's notebooks. I remind them they can't forget the comma or the FANBOYS. "You need both to create compound sentences."

After a few minutes, I ask, "How did you combine the first pair of sentences?"

Patrick raises his hand. "I wrote: *A nervous chuckle rose up in me, and I refused to let it out.*"

"Did anyone else connect the sentence with *and*?"

About two-thirds of the students raise their hands.

"Why did you use *and*, Patrick?"

"I guessed."

I have to admit, a chuckle rose up in me. "Okay, well, you guessed right. Does anybody else have a reason for choosing *and*?"

We discuss how writers may choose to connect two equal ideas. I ask students which of the other FANBOYS they tried. *But, yet,* and *so* work; however, *or, nor,* and *for* don't. We discuss how the other connectors function: *or* gives us a choice, *but* and *yet* show contrast, *so* and *for* show cause-effect relationships, and *nor* is a negative form of *or*. There is plenty to discuss, of course. We don't have to discuss everything all at once, nor should we.

Combining sentences, uncombining, and recombining all combine to bring playfulness and discovery into the process of learning to edit and write effectively. If that's not inviting, then what is?

9.6 *Invitation* to Celebrate

We tape sentence strips with compound sentences up all around the room. For homework kids read—or shop—the world, looking for compound sentences in

- their science or social studies book;
- advertisements;
- other people's speech.

Or maybe they will make one up. I give them note cards to record the discoveries they make in their daily lives. Building on the shopping metaphor, we see the concept applied, and we continue to clarify it. Posting these finds on the wall keeps our pattern growing. We discuss the "compound-sentence test" when we have near-misses. Now students are ready to reenter an essay or writer's notebook entry and see if they have some sentences to combine. We can continue the conversation about why we use compound sentences.

9.7 *Invitation* to Edit

> *He yelped in pain, and she grabbed his wrists and pinned his arms to the floor.*
> —Brian Selznick, *The Invention of Hugo Cabret* (2007)

I begin by showing the book *The Invention of Hugo Cabret.* I show them a few pages and share how cool I think this hybrid novel–picture book is. Hugo has this secret that he is trying to keep, and this girl he knows a little followed him and is about to discover his secret. Hugo fights to keep his secret undiscovered, but Isabelle starts to fight back: *He yelped in pain, and she grabbed his wrists and pinned his arms to the floor.*

Figure 9.3

UNCOVERING HOW WRITERS COMMUNICATE WITH READERS

How'd They Do It?

He yelped in pain, and she grabbed his wrists and pinned his arms to the floor.
—Brian Selznick, *The Invention of Hugo Cabret* (2007)

He yelped in pain, and she grabbed his wrists and pinned his arms the floor.

He yelps in pain, and she grabs his wrists and pins his arms to the floor.

He yelped in pain, and she grabed his wrists and pinned his arms to the floor.

He yelped in pain and she grabbed his wrists and pinned his arms to the floor.

He yelped in pain, and she grabbed his wrists, and pinned his arms to the floor.

After the correct sentence is shown, students identify changes as each subsequent sentence is uncovered separately. We are open to changes from sentence to sentence so that the activity continues to be generative.

We discuss all the things we notice as usual—commas, conjunctions, powerful verbs, and so on. Then I cover the published sentence and show it again with one change. *He yelped in pain, and she grabbed his wrists, and pinned his arms to the floor.*

I added a comma because a common mistake students make is using a comma every time they see a coordinating conjunction or FANBOY—such as the second *and* in this sentence. A student points this change out, and we discuss how *and pinned his arms to the floor* is a "poser" compound. It looks like another compound sentence because it has an *and* dividing up sentence parts. "Why isn't it another compound sentence?"

"There isn't a subject," Jose offers (after I drop a lot of hints).

It takes a subject and a verb to make a sentence. We are reviewing, building concepts, and developing their writer's eye. Then I uncover the sentence, making one more change each time. The beauty is that I can make any change or highlight any concept I want. Review or introduce, it's up to me. I can deal with subject-verb agreement, prepositions, possessive pronouns, or spelling (see Figure 9.3).

9.8 Extending the Invitation

The Schwa was right beside them, but nobody could see him.
—Jaimie, in response to *The Schwa Was Here*

When we read in my class, I sometimes ask students to use a pattern that we have learned or are learning to express their thinking about something we've read or learned in class. After reading a chapter of *The Schwa Was Here* (2006) by Neal Shusterman, I asked the students to respond to the reading by writing a compound sentence about an important occurrence in the chapter. Jaime used the correct form. The next day I put up several of the correct sentences and we used them as a review of what we had read so far, as well as a review of the compound sentence. This strategy works surprisingly well with most concepts of editing, and once again, we see grammar and editing as a way to shape and express our thoughts.

10

What's Up?
Teaching Dialogue

INTRODUCTION

What you want students to walk away knowing about dialogue:

- Dialogue moves a narrative along and/or reveals something about a character.
- We indent every time a new person speaks.
- The end punctuation goes inside quotation marks.
- Dialogue can help us show rather than tell.
- *Said* is not dead.

Misunderstandings that may need clarification:

- Retelling dialogue exactly instead of just giving your reader the good stuff
- Summarizing dialogue all the time instead of letting the characters say it
- Thinking summarizing is always wrong instead of sometimes using it to keep the story moving
- Using too many creative words to mean *said*

Dialogue reveals character and creates distinctive voice. Teachers want it. Readers crave it. But how do those authors do it? They use their ears to see how people talk, and they use contractions to sound real. But what else?

This unit of editing study connects nicely to the unit on paragraphing—"Indent every time a new person speaks" really means "Start a new paragraph every time a new person speaks." Lessons explore these questions: Is *said* dead or did you just twitter? Can dialogue float on the page without anything tethering it to movement and description? For how long?

Say What?

Dialogue versus Dialog. Yep, it can be spelled both ways—and still be correct. Dialogue: It's what people say . . . and so is *dialog*.

Attributions or **dialogue tags**: It's all a matter of *he said, she said*.

INVITATIONS

10.1 *Invitation* to Notice

"Everything we eat tonight has a special meaning," Dad said. "These vegetables mean wealth."

"How about the shrimp?" I asked.

"That means wealth, too," Dad said.

"What does pork mean?" Lissy asked.

"Wealth too!" Dad said.

"Everything means wealth," Lissy said. "All we care about is money!"

"Well, don't you want to be rich?" Mom asked.

"Yes!" Lissy said.

"Me, too," Ki-Ki said. "Me, too."

"Well, eat these," Mom told us, passing us the fried dumplings. "They say they symbolize gold coins, so if you eat them you'll be rich."

"I don't know how they're going to make me rich," I said. "They don't look like gold coins to me."

"Maybe that's what coins looked like in the olden days," Lissy whispered to me.

"I'm going to eat all of them," Dad teased, "then I'll have all the money and you'll have none."

"That's not fair," I said, trying to grab some dumplings off his plate. "Give me some."

"I'll sell you one for a dollar," Dad said. "That's how you get rich!"

The phone rang again and this time it was Grandpa calling to say Happy New Year.

"I'll bet Grandpa ate a lot of these dumplings," Lissy said. "Grandpa's rich."

"Maybe he charged two dollars for each dumpling," I joked.

—Grace Lin, *The Year of the Dog* (2007)

I turn on the overhead, illuminating the passage from *The Year of the Dog*. I ask, "What do you notice?"

"They're talking and eating."

"Yes, they are. What else?"

Lacrisha points out that several people are talking, and I ask how we can tell which one is talking when. We reread and discuss what we see.

I explain to students that I have learned to really pay attention to dialogue—or people talking, for that matter. I pay attention to how authors write dialogue. I listen extra carefully to conversations. I keep asking myself: "How do they talk to each other?"

I pick up my copy of *Bird by Bird* (1995) and explain that writer Anne Lamott gives us some tips about writing dialogue: "Good dialogue encompasses both what is said and not said."

"That gets me thinking." I repeat the quote. "What do you think she means?"

After our discussion, I sum it up or enhance it with a few closing comments. "So, we know that writing dialogue is not only about giving people things to say, but also about the actions they do while they are talking. That's a good start. Let's watch how writers sprinkle actions in. Grace Lin did this in her book *The Year of the Dog*."

This time I make a transparency of the text and students help me highlight with overhead pens. First we read the text, and then we go through it line by line, marking actions in red and dialogue in blue.

"Hey, I notice something in this part near the end," I say.

The phone rang again and this time it was Grandpa calling to say Happy New Year.

"I'll bet Grandpa ate a lot of these dumplings," Lissy said. "Grandpa's rich."

"Here we don't hear Grandpa's voice," I say. "Lin explains or summarizes. How would it be different if she went through the whole dialogue with Grandpa?"

"Well, you wouldn't be able to hear him if he were on the phone," Angel offers.

"You know, I hadn't thought of that, Angel, but you're right. What else?"

"It might get boring if she said everything everybody said. It's like the brushing-your-teeth thing in the leads," Jasmin says. She remembers that we begin our writing with the important action. Just because we are writing about an important day doesn't mean we write about brushing our teeth that day. That's not part of the important-day focus.

I bring the conversation around to the fact that writers are selective. "They choose to write only about what's important. They delete things that don't move the story along." I pause. "What if she went through every bit of the dinner, describing every—I mean every—detail?" The phone conversation might go like this:

"Hello."
"This is Grandpa," Grandpa said.
"Hey, Grandpa."

I think aloud, "We don't even have to know who answered the phone. We should probably leave some things out too. Maybe that's the *not-said* part that Anne Lamott was writing about."

Over the next few days, I hand out additional passages from stories we've already read throughout the year. Students see what else we notice and highlight different aspects of the passages, always focusing on what we notice about effective writing, not just the mechanics and style of dialogue. I also like to have different groups practice reading them aloud to pay attention to the cues the writer gives us on how we should read.

10.2 *Invitation* to Write

I distribute a copy of the passage from Grace Lin's *The Year of the Dog*. I reread the passage aloud. We discuss a few questions:

What's the setting?

What are the characters doing?

What are they talking about?

How does the writer use punctuation to shape the dialogue?

THE ELEMENTS OF DIALOGUE

Setting	Characters	Discussion	Punctuation
• Their house • Kitchen or dining room	• Talking • Eating	• Getting rich • What foods symbolize	• Quotation marks go around what's said aloud. • Indent every time a new person speaks. • Put end punctuation inside quotation marks. • Set off dialogue tags (attributions) with punctuation (mostly commas, but sometimes question or exclamation marks).

Students capture their noticings about the passage from *The Year of the Dog* on butcher paper. They will refer again to the chart in the invitation to imitate.

Figure 10.1

I list student responses in a chart on some butcher paper (see Figure 10.1). I always have to nudge this conversation along to come to these conclusions, pointing to things if they don't notice and asking questions. "I notice that here she indents and Dad's talking and then when the narrator asks a question, it indents again. And look what happens here." We keep looking as I lead them to the generalizations. I want it to come from them, but that doesn't mean I can't nudge them along.

10.3 *Invitation* to Imitate

"Sometimes we get inspired to try things authors do, and sometimes we get ideas from an author's setting or action. I keep thinking about how Grace Lin wrote about her family sitting around a table eating. It reminds me that the way we ate dinner was different. Does anybody's family eat around a table?"

"Only when we eat out," Lauren says.

"For some reason, when we eat with people, we love to talk—even though our mouths are already busy eating," I offer.

Figure 10.2

INVITATION TO PERSUADE

I always look for opportunities for my students to write persuasively. I found a picture book titled *Hey, Little Ant,* by Phillip and Hanna Hoose (1998), that invites students to persuade at the end. The story is told through dialogue. A boy spots an ant on the sidewalk and tells the ant he is going to squish it, and the ant begs him not to. The dialogue goes back and forth until the book concludes with a question: "Should the ant get squished? Should the ant go free?" The students end the book and explain why they make the choice to squish or not to squish.

"Sometimes," Andrew adds, "I don't even get to eat my lunch because I can't stop talking."

We look again at what we learned from Lin's passage (Figure 10.1) and at the copies of the passage I handed out before. We are going to imitate Lin by writing about eating and talking.

"Does it have to be at home?"

"No, you can write about any place you talk and eat. You just need to use dialogue." When students say they can't remember exactly what was said, it's a good moment to teach that we don't want to record everything that was said like a tape recorder. We use what's important, what we recall, but we have to shape it, make it sound like the people we eat with, talking about the same things we always talk about.

Using the chart and the passage for punctuation imitation, students write about eating with their friends in the cafeteria, using dialogue and descriptions of what they ate.

Students share with partners.

Figure 10.2 shares a way of practicing dialogue and persuasion using a picture book.

10.4 *Invitation* to Edit

"Are you a Coke person or a Pepsi person?" said Cracked-Up Katie.
Fresca was Ingrid's drink, but she said, "Pepsi."
—Peter Abrahams, *Down the Rabbit Hole* (2006)

I put the sentence on the overhead and ask Ralphie to read it.

"What are you—a Coke person or a Pepsi person?" Ralphie reads.

Of course we have to talk about that for a while.

It's not part of my plan, but as part of theirs, we decide to rewrite a Texas version—but first we look carefully at several versions of the sentence in "How'd They Do That?" (See Figure 10.3.)

I print a transparency with multiple versions of one sentence (see Figure 10.3). The sentence should be well written and review the concept we are learning, exploring what strategies communicate what to readers. I start the list with one correctly written sentence. Then I cut and paste the sentence below the correct sentence several times, changing one thing each time. I take out craft, punctuation, usage, and grammar. Students describe how the meaning or clarity changes and what we could do to make the meaning clear and effective.

Figure 10.3

UNCOVERING HOW WRITERS COMMUNICATE WITH READERS

How'd They Do It?

"Are you a Coke person or a Pepsi person?" said Cracked-Up Katie. Fresca was Ingrid's drink, but she said, "Pepsi."
—Peter Abrahams, *Down the Rabbit Hole* (2006)

"Are you a coke person or a Pepsi person?" said Cracked-Up Katie. Fresca was Ingrid's drink, but she said, "Pepsi."

"Are you a Coke person or a Pepsi person," said Cracked-Up Katie. Fresca was Ingrid's drink, but she said, "Pepsi."

"Are you a Coke person or a Pepsi person?" said Cracked-Up Katie. Fresca was Ingrid's drink, but she said, "Pepsi".

"Are you a Coke person or a Pepsi person?" said Cracked-Up Katie. Fresca was Ingrid's drink, but she say, "Pepsi."

After seeing the correct sentence, students identify what has changed as each subsequent sentence is uncovered separately. We are open to changes from sentence to sentence so that the activity continues to be generative.

I start by covering up all the sentences except the first, correct version. I ask, "What do you notice?" Next I cover up all versions except the one below the first one and ask students what has changed. We discuss the change, what effect it has, and how we could make the sentence better.

I repeat the process, covering and uncovering, asking what they notice, the effect of the changes, and what they'd do to improve it. I sum up the learning by showing the correct version again at the end.

Finally, we remember to write our Texas version:

> *"Are you a Big Red person or a Dr. Pepper person?" asked Put-Together Patty.*
> *Orange Crush was Dulce's drink, but she said, "Big Red."*

The next day, when students arrive, the song "That's What I Say" by Ray Charles is blasting from my iPod. I know the good feelings the music evokes will help me with my lesson. Music adds an edge of joy to editing. In this invitation to edit, I include a "How'd They Do That?" activity. Because of the length of dialogue exchanges in general, I choose to add an additional activity to edit.

> *"Wanna do something neat?"*
> *"Yeah, but just a sec. I gotta go to the bathroom."*
> *"That's the neat thing," he says. "Go there." He pointed to the four-by-five heat-register grate in the middle of the living-room floor.*
> *"Huh-uh," I say. "You'll tell."*
> *"Promise I won't," he says. "Wait till you see what happens. It's really neat."*
> *By now I have to go so bad I'm dizzy and only my death grip is stopping me from peeing into the wall like a strip miner.*
> *"Just take off your pants and pee down the grate," he says. "I promise I won't tell. I'd do it myself, but I don't have to go."*
> *"Have you ever done it before?"*
> *"Lots of times," he says. "And see? I never got in trouble for it."*
> *"No, siree . . ."*
> *"You'll be sorry if you don't. It's really neat."*
> *"Okay, but you promise you won't tell."*
> *He crosses his black heart.*
> *The same nanosecond my pee hits that hot furnace, the yellow steam rolls up around me like I'm Mandrake the Magician in the middle of a dis-*

appearing act, which I'm not but really wish I was. I know instantly from
the sssssssss and the horrific stench . . .
— Chris Crutcher, *King of the Mild Frontier* (2003)

I begin by explaining that a heat register is like heater in the floor. It blows
the hot air into the room. After reading the passage twice, I ask, "What sticks
with you from this passage?"

"It's hilarious!" Ozzie says.

"Why was it funny?"

"It sounds real. That's how I am to my little brother."

We return to the butcher paper in Figure 10.1 and add one thing: *The dia-*
logue sounds like real people talking. Then we discuss how the Crutcher passage follows the same patterns as other passages we have analyzed.

I turn off the overhead and give students a copy of the passage with all the
indentations removed from the dialogue as well as some of the dialogue outside the quotation marks. "We're going to take this passage and make it use
the patterns we have been discussing over the past few days," I say. I point to
the chart. "We can use the chart for guidance." (See Figure 10.1.)

I model with a short passage how to mark the paragraph, shaping it to
show how the dialogue should be laid out and sound:

"Wanna do something neat" "Yeah, but just a sec. I gotta go to the bath-
room" "That's the neat thing," he says. "Go there." He pointed to the four-
by-five heat-register grate in the middle of the living-room floor.

We mark:

¶ *"Wanna do something neat?" ¶ "Yeah, but just a sec. I gotta go to the*
bathroom." ¶ "That's the neat thing," he says. "Go there." He pointed to
the four-by-five heat-register grate in the middle of the living-room floor.

Then we rewrite it on notebook paper and it looks like this:

    "Wanna do something neat?"
    "Yeah, but just a sec. I gotta go to the bathroom."
    "That's the neat thing," he says. "Go there." He pointed to the four-
by-five heat-register grate in the middle of the living-room floor.

I retype the passage from *King of the Mild Frontier*, taking out all the indentions (see Figure 10.4). I leave it to groups to edit or revise this passage,

Figure 10.4

INDENTION AS REVISION

"Wanna do something neat?" "Yeah, but just a sec. I gotta go to the bathroom." "That's the neat thing," he says. "Go there." He pointed to the four-by-five heat-register grate in the middle of the living-room floor. "Huh-uh," I say. "You'll tell." "Promise I won't," he says. "Wait till you see what happens. It's really neat." By now I have to go so bad I'm dizzy and only my death grip is stopping me from peeing into the wall like a strip miner. "Just take off your pants and pee down the grate," he says. "I promise I won't tell. I'd do it myself, but I don't have to go." "Have you ever done it before?" "Lots of times," he says. "And see? I never got in trouble for it." "No, siree . . ." "You'll be sorry if you don't. It's really neat." "Okay, but you *promise* you won't tell." He crosses his black heart. The same nanosecond my pee hits that hot furnace, the yellow steam rolls up around me like I'm Mandrake the Magician in the middle of a disappearing act, which I'm not but *really* wish I was. I know instantly from the *sssssssss* and the horrific stench . . ."

After partners edit the passage, they rewrite it on notebook paper, indenting and adding punctuation when necessary.

---

making decisions about what goes where, using the pilcrow to mark the divisions. While they work, I play Ray Charles again.

After students revise and edit the passage, we share our answers, comparing and contrasting our reasoning and the effect on comprehension and sound. We compare it with a transparency of the actual text, focusing on any points of contention that arose during the discussion of their paragraphing choices.

10.5 *Invitation* to Revise

And when he'd waded out a safe distance, he sat down in the water and called, "Okay, now look!" Then he stuck a finger up in the air like he had before and waited. Only instead of gas bubbles coming to the surface, he came shooting out of the water like a torpedo, screaming like he's gonna die.

And then I saw it—a flashy, silvery, spiky-finned crappie chompin' down on his privates.

"Do something! Do something!" Joey screamed, flailing around, falling in the water, standing up, falling down, while the crappie hung on like it had struck the mother lode.

I didn't know how I was going to help, but I jumped in the pool anyway. But by the time I'd made it over to him, Joey had struck a finger through that crappie's gill and set himself free.

I tried not to look, but Joey was red, boy. Red and raw. He hurled the crappie way up onshore, then eased back into the water, whimpering and quivering, his eyes brimming with tears.

"You want me to get a doctor?" I whispered.

"No!"

"Did he . . . did he get any of it?"

"No!"

I stood there just waiting while he tried to ease the pain, but finally I couldn't help looking around the pond and asking, "What if there's more of 'em?"

He shot out of the water and dived for shore, holding himself safe the whole time. And after I'd left him alone to inspect himself for a minute, I tried asking again, "You sure you don't want to go to the doctor?"

He stepped into his skivvies and tucked himself away real careful-like before putting on his jeans. "No. What would he do to it, huh? I don't want no doctor bandaging me." Then he put on this shirt and said, "I swear to howdy, if you ever tell a soul . . ."

—Wendelin Van Draanen, *Swear to Howdy* (2003)

We have worked on chunking dialogue, by breaking it up with a new line—or paragraph—every time a new person speaks. We have also begun intentionally noticing the actions that float between the actual words said aloud that end up within the quotation marks.

Before I share the original passage from *Swear to Howdy*, students need some setup. It's summer and two boys have struck up a friendship. One friend wants to teach the other a thing or two about life—like how to fart. By the way, you might not like this passage. Another will do, but you're guaranteed to get a lot of laughs and get the kids' attention. In any case, they are at the river and he is trying to teach his friend the fine art of farting underwater and making bubbles—a worthy pursuit. As the scene opens, he is giving one of his numerous lessons on farting, but this will surely be his last. You also need to know that crappies are a kind of fish.

Figure 10.5

SWEAR TO HOWDY LIGHT

"Okay, now look!"

"Do something! *Do* something!"

"You want me to get a doctor?"

"No!"

"Did he . . . did he get *any* of it?"

"No!"

 "What if there's more of 'em?"

"You sure you don't want to go to the doctor?"

"No. What would he do to it, huh? I don't want no doctor bandaging me."

 "I swear to howdy, if you ever tell a soul . . ."

The Talking Heads might be a good rock band; however, talking heads—or quotations floating across the page without tags or action to ground them in a setting or give them a context—make it problematic for a reader to visualize and understand.

I read the passage aloud, asking kids to predict along the way.

"What if . . ." I pause. "What if Wendelin Van Draanen wrote only dialogue?" Blank stares.

I give them a copy of the passage without anything except the actual dialogue—the words that would be said aloud, like an audio recording (see Figure 10.5). I ask, "What do you think of this?"

"It's like . . . I don't know . . . stuff is missing," Joshua says.

Turning toward the class, I say, "What stuff's missing?"

"The in-between stuff," says Vanessa.

"Turn to your group and discuss what in-between stuff is missing." Vanessa asks to see the original text. I put the transparency of the original text I had prepared. Anytime I read something aloud, I try to make a transparency of it, if only to look at it at some point later.

Groups share what is missing. I probe until they get very specific, even asking them to read. Students turn back to their groups and try to summarize what "all the in-between stuff" is made up of. We share and I collect our thinking on a piece of butcher paper that will stay up as long as there is space—maybe moving to the hall after that.

10.6 *Extending* the Invitation

Is *said* really dead? If so, we need to work our magic and bring it back to life. But did it ever die? Look in a book—any book. You will see the evidence. You will see that *said* is alive and well and living in books and conversations. And it will be for a long time.

Dialogue tags, identifications, attributions, whatever you call them, need to be done well. Often we believe the more variety, the better: *twittered, effervesced, babbled, articulated, advised, nagged, shrieked, snarled, pledged, sassed, speculated.* Word choice, or shall I say diction, makes writing better, right?

Not so with *said. Said* sinks into the background, as it should. Yes, I am a *said* apologist. Rarely a word other than *said* works, but not often. If we rarely do something, it is emphasized. We don't want every tag to stand out. The words in between the quotation are of the utmost importance, what they reveal about characters, how they move the story along, not how they balked, blabbed, directed, dictated, emitted, grunted, piped, related, spewed, thanked, uttered, yapped. Sometimes. Sometimes it can work—but we want the tags to fade in. Tags are utilitarian for the most part, not art. But there are some ways to make dialogue art without stammering out fancy tags.

Another way to go without the tag altogether is to use a process screenwriters use: dialogue packets.

Dialogue packets are a screenwriter's trick: Stimulus + internalization + response (Bickham 1999). Playing with dialogue packets can be fun. You work on adding detail and movement—and leaving off a tag altogether sometimes. I throw that in for all those *said* haters.

Stimulus: Something happens
Internalization: What the character thinks
Response: How the character responds to stimulus
(Sometimes we may skip the internalization.)

Luke threw his pizza crust and hit Anali between the eyes (stimulus). All the times Luke teased her rushed through her brain like a flash flood (internalization). She picked up the crust and threw it back at Luke.
  "I'm tired of you, Luke Veracruz."
  Then her French fries, her Salisbury steak, and her half-empty chocolate milk carton flew across the table, hitting a dodging Luke (response).

Invite students to try out the formula as a strategy to see what it reveals. We'd never tell kids to do this all the time, but we do use this strategy to play and to explore dialogue and ways to show rather than tell.

An Invitation for You: Keep the Conversation Flowing

Inherent in the writing and editing process are change and evolution. My students showed me the power of what can unfold from a powerful text and positive language—even around editing. My students and I no longer avoid editing; we edit every day, even if it doesn't look like the traditional way of doing it. As we teach our students to craft writing, we tell them to *show rather than tell*. I think when teaching editing well, we *show rather than correct*.

Teaching editing as a process has allowed me to:

- examine my own dialogue about editing. Do I really believe students can edit? How do I show them I believe that with the integrity of my words? Now I carefully choose the words I use to talk about editing.
- start with wonderful texts and the joy of seeing where they take us.
- be flexible about which invitations I use and when.
- celebrate all the little victories.
- continue to collect great sentences.
- compare and contrast models.
- shape editing into a problem-solving process.
- zoom in and out from the sentence level to larger texts and back.

As Donald Graves (1984) warns: "The enemy is orthodoxy." There is no one way to teach editing. We watch our students, we listen to their responses, we believe they can think and edit.

My wish is for you to take the ideas presented in this book and make editing a more invitational experience for your students. In so doing, we can shift attitudes about what editing is and the world's comfort with it as well as our own. Isn't it a worthy goal to create a world where people aren't afraid of grammar or editing? Because if we do this, in the end, kids will be freer to write and celebrate the written word—every day—one writer at a time.

References

Anderson, Jeff. 2005. *Mechanically Inclined: Building Grammar, Usage, and Style into Writer's Workshop*. Portland, ME: Stenhouse.

———. 2006. "Helping Writers Find Power." *Educational Leadership: Helping Struggling Students* 63 (5): 70–73.

———. 2006 "Zooming In and Zooming Out: Putting Grammar in Context into Context." *English Journal* 95 (5): 28–34.

Angelillo, Janet. 2002. *A Fresh Approach to Teaching Punctuation*. New York: Scholastic.

Bain, Alexander. 1866. *English Composition and Rhetoric*. New York: Appleton.

Bernabei, Gretchen. 2005. *Reviving the Essay: How to Teach Structure Without Formula*. Shoreham, VT: Discover Writing.

Bickham, Jack M. 1999. *Scene and Structure*. Cincinnati: Writer's Digest Books.

Bleich, David. 1975. *Reading and Feelings: An Introduction to Subjective Criticism*. Urbana, IL: National Council of Teachers of English.

Bryson, Bill. 1990. *The Mother Tongue: English and How It Got That Way*. New York: William Morrow.

Buckner, Aimee. 2005. *Notebook Know-How: Strategies for the Writer's Notebook*. Portland, ME: Stenhouse.

Caine, Renate N., Geoffrey Caine, Carol Lynn McClintic, and Karl J. Klimek. 2004. *12 Brain/Mind Learning Principles in Action: The Fieldbook for Making Connections, Teaching, and the Human Brain*. Thousand Oaks, CA: Corwin.

Cambourne, Brian. 1993. *The Whole Story: Natural Learning and the Acquisition of Literacy in the Classroom.* New York: Scholastic.

Carroll, Joyce Armstrong, and Edward E. Wilson. 1993. *Acts of Teaching: How to Teach Writing: A Text, A Reader, A Narrative.* Englewood, CO: Teacher Ideas.

Casagrande, June. 2006. *Grammar Snobs Are Great Big Meanies: A Guide to Language for Fun and Spite.* New York: Penguin.

Christensen, Francis, and Bonniejean Christensen. 1976. *A New Rhetoric.* New York: Harper and Row.

Covey, Stephen. 2004. *The 7 Habits of Highly Effective People.* Rev. ed. New York: Free Press.

Duncan, Mike. 2007. "Whatever Happened to the Paragraph?" *College English* 69 (5): 470–95.

Fearn, L., and N. Farnan. 2005. "An Investigation of the Influence of Teaching Grammar in Writing to Accomplish an Influence on Writing." Paper presented at the annual meeting of the American Educational Research Association, Montreal, Canada, April.

Fletcher, Ralph, and Joann Portalupi. 1998. *Craft Lessons: Teaching Writing K–8.* Portland, ME: Stenhouse.

Gallagher, Kelly. 2004. *Deeper Reading: Comprehending Challenging Texts, 4–12.* Portland, ME: Stenhouse.

Graham, Steve, and Dolores Perin. 2007. *Writing Next: Effective Strategies to Improve Writing of Adolescents in Middle and High Schools—A Report to Carnegie Corporation of New York.* Washington, DC: Alliance for Excellent Education.

Graves, Donald. 1984. "The Enemy Is Orthodoxy." In *A Researcher Learns to Write.* Portsmouth, NH: Heinemann.

Johnston, Peter H. 2004. *Choice Words: How Our Language Affects Children's Learning.* Portland, ME: Stenhouse.

Lamott, Anne. 1994. *Bird by Bird.* New York: Pantheon.

Marzano, Robert J., Debra J. Pickering, and Jane E. Pollock. 2004. *Classroom Instruction That Works: Research-Based Strategies for Increasing Student Achievement.* Upper Saddle River, NJ: Prentice Hall.

Morgan, Bruce, and Deb Odom. 2004. *Writing Through the Tween Years: Supporting Writers, Grades 3–6.* Portland, ME: Stenhouse.

Morris, Alana. 2005. *Vocabulary Unplugged.* Shoreham, VT: Discover Writing.

Murray, Donald M. 2003. *A Writer Teaches Writing.* 2nd ed. Boston: Heinle.

Noden, Harry R. 1999. *Image Grammar: Using Grammatical Structures to Teach Writing.* Portsmouth, NH: Heinemann.

Overmeyer, Mark. 2005. *When Writer's Workshop Isn't Working: Answers to Ten Tough Questions, Grades 2–5.* Portland, ME: Stenhouse.

Peck, Robert Newton. 1988. *Secrets of Successful Fiction.* Seattle, WA: Romar Books.

Piaget, Jean, and Barbel Inhelder. 2000. *The Psychology of a Child.* New York: Basic Books.

Prose, Francine. 2006. *Reading Like a Writer: A Guide for People Who Love Books and for Those Who Want to Write Them.* New York: HarperCollins.

Purkey, William Watson, and Paula Helen Stanley. 1991. *Invitational Teaching, Learning, and Living.* Washington, DC: National Education Association Professional Library.

Rodgers, Paul. 1966. "A Discourse-Centered Rhetoric of the Paragraph." *College Composition and Communication* 17:2–11.

Spandel, Vicki. 2004. *Creating Writers Through 6-Trait Writing Assessment and Instruction.* 4th ed. Boston: Allyn and Bacon.

Stiggins, Richard J. 2000. *Student-Involved Classroom Assessment.* Upper Saddle River, NJ: Prentice Hall.

Tomlin, Lily. 2003. *The Best of Lily Tomlin.* Audio CD. Polydor.

Vygotsky, Lev. 1986. *Thought and Language.* Cambridge, MA: MIT Press.

Weaver, Constance. 1996. *Teaching Grammar in Context.* Portsmouth, NH: Boynton/Cook.

Literature

Abbott, Tony. 2007. *Firegirl.* New York: Little, Brown Young Readers.

Abrahams, Peter. 2006. *Down the Rabbit Hole.* New York: HarperTrophy.

———. 2007. *Nerve Damage: A Novel.* New York: William Morrow.

Acampora, Paul. 2006. *Defining Dulcie.* New York: Dial.

Almond, Steve. 2005. *Candyfreak: A Journey Through the Chocolate Underbelly of America.* New York: Harvest Books.

Anderson, Laurie Halse. 2001. *Speak.* New York: Puffin.

Angelou, Maya. 1969. *I Know Why the Caged Bird Sings.* New York: Random House.

Appelt, Kathi. 2004. *My Father's Summers: A Daughter's Memoir.* New York: Henry Holt.

Avi. 2004. *The End of the Beginning: Being the Adventures of a Small Snail (and an Even Smaller Ant).* New York: Harcourt.

Banks, Kate. 2006. *Max's Words.* New York: Farrar, Straus and Giroux.

Barenaked Ladies. 1992. "If I Had $1,000,000." From *Gordon.* CD. Sire Records.

Baylor, Byrd. 1995. *I'm in Charge of Celebrations.* New York: Aladdin.

———. 1997. *The Other Way to Listen.* New York: Aladdin.

Benchley, Peter. 2007. *Shark Life: True Stories About Sharks & the Sea.* New York: Yearling.

Best, Cari. 2003. *Three Cheers for Catherine the Great!* New York: Farrar, Straus and Giroux.

Bosquez, Mario. 2005. *The Chalupa Rules: A Latino Guide to Gringolandia.* New York: Penguin.

Byars, Betsy, Betsy Duffey, and Laurie Myers. 2004. *The SOS File.* New York: Henry Holt.

Carbone, Elisa. 2006. *Blood on the River: James Town 1607*. New York: Viking Juvenile.

Chambers, Veronica. 1998. *Marisol and Magdalena: The Sound of Our Sisterhood*. New York: Scholastic.

Choldenko, Gennifer. 2004. *Al Capone Does My Shirts*. New York: G. P. Putnam's Sons.

Cisneros, Sandra. 1991. *The House on Mango Street*. New York: Vintage.

Cleary, Beverly. 1965. *The Mouse and the Motorcycle*. New York: William Morrow.

———. 1981. *Ramona Quimby, Age 8*. New York: William Morrow.

Clements, Andrew. 1998. *Frindle*. New York: Aladdin.

———. 2004. *The Report Card*. New York: Simon and Schuster.

———. 2004. *A Week in the Woods*. New York: Scholastic.

Codell, Esme Raji. 2006. *Sing a Song of Tuna Fish: Hard-to-Swallow Stories from the Fifth Grade*. New York: Hyperion.

Crichton, Michael. 1996. *Lost World: Jurassic Park*. New York: Ballantine.

Crutcher, Chris. 2003. *King of the Mild Frontier: An Ill-Advised Biography*. New York: HarperCollins.

Dahl, Roald. 1998. *Matilda*. New York: Puffin.

Davis, Kenneth C. 2002. *Don't Know Much About the Universe: Everything You Need to Know About Outer Space but Never Learned*. New York: HarperCollins.

Degross, Monalisa. 1994. *Donavan's Word Jar*. New York: HarperCollins.

Delano, Marfé Ferguson. 2005. *Genius: A Photobiography of Albert Einstein*. Washington, DC: National Geographic Children's Books.

d'Harcourt, Claire. 2006. *Masterpieces Up Close: Western Painting from the 14th to 20th Centuries*. San Francisco: Chronicle Books.

DiTerlizzi, Tony, and Holly Black. 2003. *Lucinda's Secret (The Spiderwick Chronicles, Book 3)*. New York: Simon and Schuster.

Giles, Gail. 2004. *Dead Girls Don't Write Letters*. New York: Simon Pulse.

Gutman, Dan. 2005. "Let's Go to the Videotape." In *Guys Write for Guys Read*, ed. Jon Scieszka. New York: Viking.

Hakim, Joy. 1993. *The History of US: From Colonies to Country, 1735–1791*. New York: Oxford University Press.

Hannigan, Katherine. 2006. *Ida B. . . . and Her Plans to Maximize Fun, Avoid Disaster, and (Possibly) Save the World*. New York: HarperTrophy.

Hautman, Pete. 2004. *Godless*. New York: Simon and Schuster.

Hemingway, Ernest. 1964. *A Moveable Feast*. New York: Scribner.

Hiaasen, Carl. 2005. *Flush*. New York: Knopf.

Hinton, S. E. 1997. *The Outsiders*. New York: Puffin.

Hoose, Philip, and Hannah Hoose. 1998. *Hey, Little Ant*. Berkeley, CA: Tricycle.

Horvath, Polly. 2001. *The Trolls*. New York: Farrar, Straus and Giroux.

———. 2004. *Everything on a Waffle*. New York: Farrar, Straus and Giroux.

Howe, James. 2007. *Totally Joe*. New York: Aladdin.

Johnston, Tony. 2003. *Any Small Goodness: A Novel of the Barrio.* New York: Scholastic.

Klass, David. 2002. *You Don't Know Me.* New York: HarperTeen.

Konigsburg, E. L. 1967. *From the Mixed-Up Files of Mrs. Basil E. Frankweiler.* New York: Atheneum.

———. 1996. *The View from Saturday.* New York: Scholastic.

Korman, Gordon. 1998. *The Chicken Doesn't Skate.* New York: Hyperion.

Langley, Andrew. 2006. *Hurricanes, Tsunamis, and Other Natural Disasters.* New York: Kingfisher.

Levitt, Steven D., and Stephen J. Dubner. 2005. *Freakonomics: A Rogue Economist Explores the Hidden Side of Everything.* New York: HarperCollins.

Lin, Grace. 2007. *The Year of the Dog.* New York: Little, Brown.

Littman, Sarah. 2005. *Confessions of a Closet Catholic.* New York: Dutton.

Lord, Cynthia. 2006. *Rules.* New York: Scholastic.

Lowry, Lois. 2002. *Gooney Bird Greene.* New York: Yearling.

Lyga, Barry. 2006. *The Astonishing Adventures of Fanboy and Goth Girl.* Boston: Houghton Mifflin.

Mack, Tracy. 2002. *Drawing Lessons.* New York: Scholastic.

Mann, Aimee. 1999. "One." Soundtrack to *Magnolia.* United Musicians.

Martin, Ann M. 2005a. *A Dog's Life.* New York: Scholastic.

———. 2005b. *A Corner of the Universe.* New York: Scholastic.

Mass, Wendy. 2006. *Jeremy Fink and the Meaning of Life.* New York: Little, Brown.

McNamee, Graham. 2003. *Acceleration.* New York: Wendy Lamb Books.

Meehl, Brian. 2006. *Out of Patience.* New York: Delacorte.

Murphy, Jim. 1990. *The Boys' War: Confederate and Union Soldiers Talk About the Civil War.* New York: Scholastic.

———. 2000. *Blizzard! The Storm That Changed America.* New York: Scholastic.

———. 2003a. *Dugout Wisdom: The Ten Principles of Championship Teams.* Monterey, CA: Coaches Court.

———. 2003b. *An American Plague: The True and Terrifying Story of the Yellow Fever Epidemic of 1793.* New York: Clarion Books.

Osa, Nancy. 2003. *Cuba 15.* New York: Delacorte.

Patron, Susan. 2006. *The Higher Power of Lucky.* New York: Atheneum/Richard Jackson Books.

Payment, Simone. 2003. *Navy Seals: Special Operations for the U.S. Navy.* New York: Rosen.

Pennypacker, Sara. 2006. *Clementine.* New York: Hyperion.

Perkins, Lynne Rae. 2005. *Criss Cross.* New York: Greenwillow.

Pilkey, Dav. 2006. *Captain Underpants and the Preposterous Plight of the Purple Potty People.* New York: Scholastic.

Roberts, Diane. 2004. *Made You Look.* New York: Yearling.

Ryan, Pam Muñoz. 2004. *Becoming Naomi Leon.* New York: Scholastic.

Rylant, Cynthia. 1996. *The Old Woman Who Named Things*. San Diego, CA: Harcourt.

Savage. Jeff. 2003. *Play-by-Play Football*. Minneapolis: LernerSports.

Schaefer, Lola M. 2006. *An Island Grows*. New York: Greenwillow.

Schotter, Roni. 2006. *The Boy Who Loved Words*. New York: Schwartz and Wade.

Schwartz, Alvin. 2001. *Scary Stories 3: More Tales to Chill Your Bones*. New York: HarperCollins.

Schwartz, Amy. 1991. *Annabelle Swift, Kindergartner.* New York: Scholastic.

Scieszka, Jon. 1993. *Your Mother Was a Neanderthal*. New York: Penguin.

Selznick, Brian. 2007. *The Invention of Hugo Cabret*. New York: Scholastic.

Shinn, Sharon. 2004. *The Safe-Keeper's Secret*. New York: Viking Juvenile.

Shusterman, Neal. 2006. *The Schwa Was Here*. New York: Puffin.

Simon, Seymour. 2003. *Spiders*. New York: HarperCollins.

Smith, Roland. 2007. *Jack's Run*. New York: Hyperion.

Smith, Scott. 2006. *The Ruins*. New York: Knopf.

Spinelli, Jerry. 1991. *Fourth Grade Rats*. New York: Scholastic.

———. 2000. *Stargirl*. New York: Scholastic.

———. 2007. *Eggs*. New York: Little, Brown.

Stewart, Paul, and Chris Riddle. 1999. *Beyond the Deepwoods (The Edge Chronicles)*. London: Corgi Books.

Tishy, Cecelia. 2007. *All in One Piece*. New York: Grand Central.

Treat, Wesley, Heather Shades, and Rob Riggs. 2005. *Weird Texas*. New York: Sterling.

Van Draanen, Wendelin. 2003. *Swear to Howdy*. New York: Knopf.

Vlautin, Willy. 2007. *The Motel Life*. New York: Harper Perennial.

Westerfeld, Scott. 2005. *Uglies*. New York: Simon and Schuster.